Daytop

DAYTOP

Three Addicts and Their Cure

By Daniel Casriel, M.D., and Grover Amen

 HILL AND WANG NEW YORK

30240

Contents

Preface

Studying the latest figures on the rise of drug addiction in this country, I have been thinking, almost with nostalgia, of the era of Frankie the Greek. Frankie the Greek was an old-time addict of the days before World War Two. He was a loner, or what we psychiatrists would classify as a schizoid type. Schizoid he probably was, but he seems now to represent a type whose life-style posed little or no threat to society. He was a shadowy, elusive person of the kind legends are built around. He had no contact with his family, no close friends. He did not, so far as I know, indulge in any aggressive criminal activities aside from his addiction. During the warm months of the year, he would travel throughout the country, from town to town, practicing his trade of selling domestically made carpets, which he claimed were stolen from the Orient. He lived frugally, hoarding his profits to set up a winter store of morphine—enough to see him through the winter in Maine where he had a shack; his only other supplies were canned beans to eat and fuel oil to keep him warm. Perfectly self-sufficient with his beans and morphine, he would remain in a state of drugged, euphoric hibernation until the following spring when the snows melted and he would take to the road again as a traveling salesman.

Before the 1950's, drug addiction was not exclusively the preserve of people like Frankie the Greek. There were certain groups, such as jazz musicians, who were notorious for their use of drugs, both heroin and marijuana, but such use, even of heroin, was viewed by the general population as an activity tinged with a certain offbeat glamour. It is interesting to note that even the use of marijuana was viewed then by the middle classes in much the same light. It was almost as taboo as heroin, but because of its equally restricted use, those who smoked pot were viewed as isolated types. They were certainly not seen as a serious threat to society.

There were also practical and economic reasons behind the limited number of drug addicts prior to the end of World War Two. Addicts at that time were eager *not* to make new converts, since it threatened their own source of the drug, which was in short supply. But after World War Two, with the breakdown of international control of the drug traffic, the supply rose sharply, while the number of addicts had declined. If a profit was to be made, new markets had to be found in a hurry.

It was in the 1950's that the heroin merchants found a major market in the black ghettos of New York. The miserable slum conditions which prevailed, in contrast to the booming economy outside of the ghettos, produced a ready and ideal consumer's market for dope. As the writer and ex-addict William Burroughs has observed, you don't need to sell junk to customers. You just sell customers to junk. During this time, of course, there was no real public concern. It was not even a question of apathy. Hardly anyone outside of the ghettos was even aware that there was a problem. Those who were, saw it as being due to ignorance, poverty, the chaotic life of the ghettos—just another problem of the poor.

During those postwar years of general optimism, the average American still saw our society, exemplified by the typical middle class family, as being essentially healthy. The rest of the world might be sick or decadent, but America was still the promised land. The ideals of hard work and material prosperity were still viable. It was not until the 1960's, when the children of the post-war years reached adolescence and maturity that the hypocrisy of this view became apparent. Prosperity had only contributed to breaking up whatever ideal of closeness the American family still espoused. The old slogans of the good life were seen to be hollow. A dehumanized society characterized by emotional repression in the family, rigid, impersonal conformity in the schools, and by an emphasis on technology, degrees, the rewards of status in higher education, had produced a new generation, aware of the hypocrisy of its elders, the absence of spontaneity, warmth, directness, loving concern in their personal relationships, but equally aware, for the most part, of its own lack of options in changing such a deeply entrenched system. It is this background which produced the healthier manifestations of the Youth Movement, political and social. But it is also among this same middle class generation that addiction to heroin spread to epidemic proportions in the last decade.

This book deals mainly with the heroin addict, and it is not the place to debate the pros and cons of marijuana or LSD and their use among the supposedly healthier segments of the new generation to get "turned on" rather than "turned off." One can only say that to require any chemicals in order to get "turned on" shows that latent warmth and spontaneity are having a hard time surfacing. And the old line which divided "acid-heads" and "pot-heads" from the hard-drug users, even five years ago, is gradually disappearing. Sadly and ironically, the educational crusades against heroin in newspaper magazines and on national television seem to have aroused an interest in experimenting with heroin rather than an aversion to it.

So how bad is the drug picture in 1971? Why has there been such an increase in addiction in the last few years, as compared with the decades before that? And, granted that we are living through a period frightening in every respect, why do those who opt for hard drugs not settle instead for pot, alcohol, or pills? This is the question I am asked most frequently. Why heroin and not something else?

The question reminds me of an intelligent lawyer I know who became interested in the "problem of drug addiction" and asked if he could visit Daytop. He went to a couple of the Saturday-night open houses, talked with many of the residents, and even sat in on one of their encounter groups. When I saw him again, he said that he had found the experience very interesting. There was only one thing that bothered him. So many of the residents there kept talking about "emotional pain." What, he wanted to know, did they mean by emotional pain?

To a professional man of forty who does not know what emotional pain is, drug addiction must indeed seem a mystifying problem. But his question pinpoints the whole way in which an emotionally turned-off society conveniently tends to particularize heroin abuse as the problem when, of course, the real problem lies in society itself. Even the frequently heard fact that "drug addiction is only a symptom" tends to be misleading, since the corollary of that statement usually is that the problem lies *solely* within the personality of the addict himself. The society is healthy, just the addict is sick, and it is up to the healthy society to cure the sick addict.

A more accurate hypothesis is that it is precisely the society itself, and, on a smaller scale, the family, with its absence of close relationships, the sense of isolation, the *inability to communicate emotionally*, which directly leads to a void in which chemicals become a substitute for human feelings, emotional pleasure: love. There are other contributing factors, such as the American tradition of "getting out on one's own" as soon as possible, the affluence among the middle classes, which makes this possible, as does the automobile, and the general endorsement of chemicals in our culture, from antibiotics and tranquilizers to sleeping pills and alcohol, which are widely tolerated and used by the same older generation so quick to condemn with moral outrage the use of more dangerous drugs.

This is not the place to go into the specific physiological and psychological effects of opiates. That is a book in itself.* Suffice it to note here that morphine and its more potent derivative, heroin, constitute the ultimate painkillers and chemical

* A useful reference work is *Drug Addiction: Physiological, Psychological and Sociological Aspects* by D. P. Ausubel (Random House, 1958).

agents of euphoria—the inhibition of the self-critical faculty. Generous use of alcohol, for instance, cannot approach the euphoric effect of opiates. Alcohol, in fact, is not even a genuine euphoriant. This being the case, it is not surprising that heroin addiction is so widespread. In New York alone, the addict population is conservatively estimated at 100,000. It could be twice that. The number of addicts in the country as a whole is estimated at somewhere between 500,000 and 1,000,000. Of this number, less than 10 percent, currently, can expect to recover and resume normal lives. The remaining 90 percent will either spend most of their lives in jail or else die as derelicts.

Shocking as these figures are, they must be viewed in the light of an even more shocking statistic: that 85 percent of the population now suffers from some kind of character disorder, and the remaining 15 percent are neurotic—an exact reversal of the figures Freud cited in his day for the general population. Put briefly, the person who is in some kind of emotional pain and knows it, is the neurotic; whereas the person whose primary reaction to pain is emotional detachment and withdrawal can be classified as suffering from a character disorder. This distinction is dealt with in detail in the concluding section of the book. At this point I only want to make clear the magnitude of the emotional sickness prevalent in society as a whole, a society in which the heroin addict can be seen as a member of a minority acting out his symptoms to one specific extreme. Seen in this light, there is no particular mystery in why one person resorts to heroin, another to alcohol or pills. Given the initial predilection for emotional withdrawal, it is only a question of exposure, availability, peer group pressures or taboos that determines which drugs are used. Obviously the Nebraska housewife is not likely to shoot junk. She will settle for pills or alcohol.

The point is that the people, not the drug, constitute the real problem. Whatever the fluctuations in the international drug traffic, in the corruption or reform of local narcotics officers, in the crackdowns on smuggling into the United States, not to mention the futility of increasingly harsh penalties inflicted on drug offenders, the problem is one of demand, not supply. Lest anyone think this is merely the professional view of a psychiatrist, William Burroughs describes it with mathematical precision in his introduction to *Naked Lunch:*

> If you wish to alter or annihilate a pyramid of numbers in a serial relation, you alter or remove the bottom number. If we wish to annihilate the junk pyramid, we must start with the bottom of the pyramid: *the Addict in the Street,* and stop tilting quixotically for the "higher ups" so called, all of whom are immediately replaceable. *The addict in the street who must have junk to live is the one irreplaceable factor in the junk equation.* When there are no more addicts to buy junk there will be no junk traffic. As long as junk need exists, someone will service it.*

Unfortunately, the spread of the drug epidemic is on a scale way out of proportion to the most successful efforts to rehabilitate and cure particular addicts. It is this fact which accounts for the political and public emphasis on "getting the addict off the street." There's no doubt about it. Because of their sheer numbers, addicts *are* a public menace, accounting for over 50 percent of the crimes against persons and property in New York City. But we must be careful not to confuse steps taken to protect society from the addict (jails, the "Rockefeller program," the federal facilities in Fort Worth, Texas, and Lexington, Kentucky, and, in my opinion, methadone maintenance) with those now being taken to rehabilitate the addict himself. For this is the only realistic long-term solution to the problem, even though less than 5 percent of the addicts in New York City are in therapeutic communities today. Unfortunately, like anything else, there are good and bad therapeutic communities, and no community is any better than the dynamic it operates on and the quality of the staff which runs it. To some, "therapeutic community" is becoming a magic phrase in itself, a dangerous misconception, for it can mean that a successful community will suffer for the failings of its rivals and imitators. This is why I don't want to make any comparisons with other therapeutic communities such as Phoenix House or Odyssey House. We are

* From "Deposition: Testimony Concerning a Sickness," the Introduction to *Naked Lunch* by William S. Burroughs. Copyright © 1959 by William Burroughs. Reprinted by permission of Grove Press, Inc.

concerned here only with Daytop Village, which was the first of the second-generation communities deriving, with certain modifications, from Synanon on the West Coast.

It was in 1962 that I first went to visit Synanon. Until then, my own experience as a psychiatrist in private practice and as a court psychiatrist had convinced me that there were only two ways to deal with the heroin addict: either put him away in a hospital or jail the rest of his life, or give him all the heroin he wants. I shared the opinion then of most of my professional colleagues: that heroin addiction was incurable. If this was the common view of the medical and psychiatric community, who could blame the public for apathy, ignorance, or indifference? Until the founding of Synanon in 1958, in California, there were virtually no treatment facilities for drug addicts other than those established by the United States Public Health Service in Lexington and Fort Worth. The cure rate in those two facilities, defined as abstinence from drugs for a period of five or more years after release, has been less than 5 percent. The Rockefeller program in New York State, which has cost more than $300 million since its founding in 1966, has been an even more expensive failure.

The latest attempt by professionals to cure heroin addiction—and one that has unfortunately received extravagant publicity—is the use of methadone. It is reminiscent of the way heroin itself was used at the turn of the century to treat morphine addiction. In December 16, 1968, Doctors Vincent Dole and Marie Nyswander, the leading proponents of methadone maintenance, reported on extensive studies, involving 750 cases, in the *Journal of the American Medical Association* (Vol. 206, No. 12), and it is on the basis of such studies that New York City established a pilot methadone program which was expanded with additional funds from the state in 1970.

Dole and Nyswander themselves state in their report:

We have not, however, considered it desirable to withdraw medication from patients who are to remain in the program, since those who have been discharged have experienced a return of narcotic drug hunger after removal of the blockade, and most of them have promptly reverted to the use of heroin. It is possible that a very gradual removal of methadone from patients with several years of stable living in phase 3 might succeed, but this procedure has not yet been adequately tested.

In the same report, Dole and Nyswander also write:

> Since blockade with methadone makes heroin relatively ineffective, a patient cannot use heroin for the usual euphoria . . . He can, however, remain drug-oriented in his thinking, and be tempted to return to heroin.

And as far back as 1948, Victor H. Vogel, Harris Isbell, and Kenneth W. Chapman reported in the *Journal of the American Medical Association* (Vol. 138, December 4, 1948) in an article entitled "The Present Status of Narcotic Addiction":

> The total addiction liability to methadone is almost equal to that of morphine, although its physical liability is less. The euphoric effect of methadone on the addict (and undoubtedly in the addiction-prone person) is equal to that of morphine, so that its habituation liability is high.

As a scientist and a doctor, I can accept *any* program that has a *research* design and is *limited* in its scope, but I am utterly opposed to the indiscriminate use of methadone as a major treatment for drug addiction. Whatever the merits of the methadone program may be in "getting addicts off the street," I don't see how we, as physicians, in all good conscience, can prescribe medication which is not curative, which itself is permanently addictive, when there is indisputable evidence *that there is a cure for the disease.*

It was in 1962 that the probation department of the Brooklyn-Staten Island district of the Supreme Court received a research grant from the National Institute of Mental Health to explore the possibilities of starting a halfway house for addicts. My help was enlisted, and, in searching for a possible model on which to base such a therapeutic community, I visited Synanon in Santa Monica, California, which, under the direction of Chuck Dederich, an ex-alcoholic, was said to be having remarkable results in rehabilitating addicts. I went there as an interested skeptic. It wasn't as well known as it is today, and what I saw excited me so much that I stayed several weeks and ended up writing a book about Synanon—*So Fair a House*. Synanon was the breakthrough. Like Alcoholics Anonymous, it showed that addicts themselves, united in a common cause, under a strong leader, without the interference of so-called professionals —whether they be doctors or sincerely concerned social workers—could achieve what the professionals had termed impossible: cure, kicking the drug habit, and feeling good about it.

Following, with certain modifications, the principles of Synanon, Daytop Lodge was established on Staten Island in 1963 as a halfway house for twenty-five addicts, all of whom were on probation for felonies. Most of Synanon's early strength, however, stemmed from the powerful personality of its founder, Chuck Dederich, who presided over what was essentially a paternalistic, tribelike community. During Daytop's first year, the difficulty of finding such a strong executive director kept the new program from getting off the ground. Several men were hired for the job, but none worked out. It wasn't until 1964, when I brought in a Synanon graduate, David Deitch, as director and an ex-Synanon member, Ronald Brancato, as assistant director, that the new concept found the necessary leadership. So that women and addicts enlisting voluntarily could also be accommodated—not just those on court probation— the private corporation of Daytop Village was founded in June of 1965.

As the population of the house grew, and word of its presence and purpose got around Staten Island, Daytop began to experience the same welcome that Synanon did in its first days out in Santa Monica. "Junkies Go Home" was the theme of protest parades and picketings. Our cars were assaulted by violent demonstrators shouting obscenities. In time the hysteria subsided, and the presence of Daytop became tolerated, if not welcomed. As the population grew, and we received funds from New York State, a second house was opened in 1966 at Swan Lake, in upstate New York, and a third house in the fall of 1968 at Fourteenth Street in downtown Manhattan.

Daytop graduated 176 ex-addicts as of February, 1971, of

whom 158 remained clean of drugs. Of the eighteen failures, five returned eventually to a therapeutic community—either at Daytop or elsewhere. The graduate figure would be much higher had Daytop not gone through an almost disastrous leadership crisis in November of 1968, during which David Deitch resigned, but managed to take most of the 200 residents with him—including thirty staff members—leaving us with a staff of ten plus thirty residents. As medical superintendent, I felt that David Deitch was structuring the community in *too* paternalistic a fashion and was using an essentially therapeutic community to promulgate his own particular brand of radical politics. There was never any question of his hard work, dedication, and contribution to Daytop. Since then, though, the new directorship, first under Ronnie Brancato, and since March 1970 under Charles Devlin, has been opposed to any kind of a "personality cult" and also to any notion that Daytop should be an isolated, self-sustaining community run along principles different than, or superior to, the surrounding society. Unlike Synanon, for instance, which is self-supporting, Daytop receives 80 percent of its operating budget from state funds. Emphasis is strictly on the therapeutic process itself and on preparing graduates to resume a normal life in the community as quickly as possible. In 1971 25 percent of the graduates had taken jobs unconnected with any therapeutic community or had resumed their education; the other 75 percent were doing staff work either at Daytop or elsewhere. In February of 1971 Daytop had 402 residents and had served as the role model for the formation of several scores of other therapeutic communities.

Daytop still has its problems. Although the "cure rate" for graduates, based on the above figures, is close to 90 percent, the splittee rate—that of people who leave Daytop before graduating—is disappointing. Of a total admission figure of about 900 between January of 1969, when Daytop reorganized after David Deitch left, and February of 1971, over 450 had left without returning. In other words, slightly less than 50 percent of those who entered Daytop either graduated or were still in the program as of February 1971.

An important factor here is certainly the low ratio of staff to residents: 1:22. All indications are that, as this ratio is raised, the splittee rate will decline accordingly. My own recent experience confirms this. I left Daytop as medical superintendent in March 1970 to found a privately supported rehabilitation center called AREBA. There our staff-to-resident ratio is 1:5, and the splittee rate over a period of one year was less than 8 percent. Our hope is that such smaller communities—the population of AREBA in February of 1971 was only thirty-four (two graduated and three left; one after one night, one after ten days, one after four months)—can serve as pilot projects for streamlining and refining the techniques employed at Daytop. Already at AREBA we have been able to reduce the time spent before graduation from Daytop's average—eighteen months to two years—down to nine months. At AREBA I have also been able to employ a detoxifying drug developed by Dr. Emanuel Revici, which eliminates almost all withdrawal symptoms during a seven-day period, and almost all subsequent physiological craving for heroin. This drug, called Perse, bears no relation to methadone. It is not a substitute for heroin, not a maintenance drug. It is a detoxifying agent which neutralizes the overactive defensive cellular response which the body builds up during prolonged heroin intake. After three days of intermuscular injection, Perse can be given effectively in tablet form. After working with Perse for over a year, I feel it represents a major medical breakthrough and should greatly facilitate the psychological treatment of addicts without using any other drugs, especially narcotics like methadone.

The concluding section of this book presents a more objective and detailed analysis of the Daytop *concept* at work, along with the psychodynamic theory behind it. First we have the stories of three ex-addicts who have since graduated from Daytop. Two held staff positions in Daytop in 1971, and the third was directing a smaller therapeutic community in upstate New York. Previous books on therapeutic communities, such as my own *So Fair a House: The Story of Synanon* and Lewis Yablonsky's *The Tunnel Back*, have dealt with the subject from a professional standpoint, the residents themselves being represented only by brief case histories. Here our intention is to acquaint both interested professionals and the general public with the human quality of the therapeutic community through the experiences of the people in it. To insure an appropriate and honest objectivity we entrusted this task to a professional writer who lived at Daytop and who was not restricted in either his choice of subjects or the presentation of their material. Consequently, some aspects of Daytop give a less favorable impression than would have been the case if this book had been an "inside job" with the self-image Daytop presents being our primary concern. It is the dynamic process which counts, and this will, as I've indicated, evolve and be modified in the years ahead as practical experience dictates. Even now it is abundantly clear that the process produces individuals not only free of drugs but liberated in a way that is rare under the best circumstances. And statistics alone will never tell that side of the story.

DANIEL CASRIEL, M.D.

Introduction

A NEW PROSPECT is brought into the interview room. His name is Victor. He's been waiting in the prospect chair for five hours. He is introduced to the six members of the interview group, who tell him to sit down; they form a semicircle around him. He looks scared, but he's doing his best to appear very calm and collected. When offered a cigarette, he declines. He is asked by the group leader, Greg, why he wants to get into Daytop. He replies that it's so he can *stay* off drugs.

"You mean you don't have a habit as of now?"

"No."

"How long have you been clean?"

"Over ten days now."

"You haven't had any drugs at all for ten days?"

"That's right."

"How long were you strung out before that?"

"A year or two—closer to two years. I shot dope sometimes before that, but I was only strung out for the last two years."

"How do you feel now?"

"Good."

Greg shrugs his shoulders and lights a cigarette. "I don't see that you have a problem," he tells Victor. "You've kicked a two-year habit in ten days all on your own, and you feel fine. What do you need Daytop for? You'd just be wasting two years of your life here."

"Two years?" asks Victor. "I understood that the program only took eighteen months."

"You understood wrong. There's no guarantee. It might be two years. And it's rough here. You don't just lay back and take it easy, like you do in the joint. Have you ever served time?"

"No."

"Ever been arrested?"

"Not until recently."

"You mean you've got a charge hanging over you?"

"Yeah. But my lawyer's pretty sure it will be dismissed."

"And this charge has nothing to do with you wanting to get into Daytop?"

"No. I just figure it's time I started doing something for myself."

This prompts a collective groan of disbelief from the group, and Greg shouts at Victor: "You lying bastard! You dishonest motherfucker! You really expect us to buy that bullshit? You're here because you're scared you just might not beat that rap. But as long as you're at Daytop you can count on a suspended sentence or at least a postponement. How about that? And there's something else. I don't buy for one second that you've been clean for ten days. You're high on something right now. I know it, and everyone else in the room knows it. When did you have your last fix?"

Before Victor can assemble his defenses, everyone begins tearing into him, and he looks around toward the door, as though he might try making a break for it. But after about twenty minutes of outraged denials and protestations, he finally breaks down and admits that he's been on Dolophines—methadone tablets—for the last ten days. "I didn't mention it because I thought it was all right," he explains. "They're legal and were prescribed by a private physician."

"Do you have any on you now?"

"No. I threw them away before coming."

xx

"That's interesting. If you thought they were all right, then why did you throw them away?"

They have him again, and the inquisition intensifies until after another half-hour he finally cops to everything, including the fact that he's been taking Seconals, prescribed by another doctor, along with the methadone; that he doesn't really want to give up heroin, just cut down on the size of his habit; and that he wouldn't be at Daytop, applying for admission, if he didn't have a charge of narcotics possession in New Jersey hanging over him. (Narcotics charges in New Jersey are harder to beat than in New York State, and the sentences, on conviction, more severe.)

"We don't give a shit what you did before you came here," Greg tells him. "All we ask is that you try to be honest, hard as that may be. Listen. You didn't do too bad. It takes some guys three hours to even admit they *like* shooting dope. What we want from you now is to make some kind of investment."

Victor says that he has a little money in the bank, but that he hopes to save it for getting back on his feet, once he's graduated from Daytop.

That gets a good laugh out of everybody.

"You can keep your money in the bank," Greg says. "But congratulations! You're the first addict I've ever met with money in the bank. What we want from you now is more an emotional investment—like just asking for help."

"How do I do that?"

"Just say it: *I need help.*"

"I need help," says Victor, but without much conviction.

"Louder," shouts the group. "We want to hear you."

It comes out louder this time, but more like a statement of defiance than a cry of distress.

"*Do* you need help?"

"Yes."

"Then shout it over and over until we can feel it. And look at each one of us as you say it."

Once he starts looking around the room, at each person, some resistance in him begins to crack. He's still fighting it, but he does manage to get the words out with a semblance of sincerity:

"I need help." And they keep him saying it, over and over, encouraging his feelings, not just the words, to come out, until soon he has dropped the ritual phrase and is just yelling the one word, "Help," and you can see that he means it, and now there are tears in his eyes he's fighting back, and everyone is standing up around him, shaking his hand and embracing him, and welcoming him as a new member of the Daytop family. As he leaves the room, he doesn't look scared any more.

That's how a new prospect gets admitted to Daytop following an initial screening at one of Daytop's three neighborhood SPAN offices—two in New York City and one in Westchester County. In the eighteen to twenty-four months that follow, the therapeutic process he experiences has but one goal, not just to produce an individual who no longer craves drugs, but to break down the insulation, the armor of withdrawal which has sealed him off not only from others, but, more importantly, from himself. As the Daytop philosophy, which is read every day at morning meeting, puts it:

"We are here because there is no refuge, finally, from ourselves. Until a person confronts himself in the eyes and hearts of others, he is running. Until he suffers them to share his secrets, he has no safety from them. Afraid to be known, he can know neither himself nor any other—he will be alone.

"Where else but in our common grounds can we find such a mirror? Here, together, a person can at last appear clearly to himself, not as the giant of his dreams or the dwarf of his fears, but as a man—part of a whole, with his share in its purpose. In this ground, we can each take root and grow, not alone any more, as in death, but alive to ourselves and to others."

Before getting to know the three people that this book is about, I lived for six weeks at the three Daytop houses. There is one on Staten Island, another at Fourteenth Street in Manhattan, and a third at Swan Lake in upstate New York. During my first week, I made many of the same mistakes that other new residents make, but my status as a resident guest kept me from getting a shaved head or wearing a sign—two of the most common disciplinary measures or "learning experiences" doled out for infractions of the house rules. To begin with, I found myself instinctively identifying with the newer residents of the house who were still on shaky grounds emotionally and therefore more disposed to rap with me in a nostalgic fashion about their experiences on the street. This didn't seem important to me at the time, but nothing at Daytop is unimportant. When morale is high or, as they say at Daytop, when the house is tight, the smallest gesture or comment is subject to scrutiny, and nobody "gets away" with anything. During a cop-out session run one night by the director of Daytop—a cop-out session being a general meeting of all residents in which guilt of all kinds is copped to, from that over stealing a cookie to that of planning to split—nine residents copped to talking negative with me, and I ended up having to cop to my own share of the lunacy. I admitted that, in my desire to be accepted in the house, I'd related to people on a superficial and negative level by talking about my experiences, not with heroin, but with pot, sleeping pills, and LSD. I was told that I would have to get out of the house if this ever happened again, that it was precisely negative small talk like that which gets the newer residents, already unsure of themselves, to thinking about splitting. Later, in encounter groups, which are one of the prime therapeutic tools at Daytop, I was shown how I was afraid to reveal my real personal emotions for fear of being rejected, that I was hiding my own shyness by coming on behind this "acid-head" image. It is impossible to be at Daytop very long and not get involved, since the overcoming of shyness, distrust, hostility, aloofness, withdrawal—all the negative stances characterized by the Daytop word "encapsulation"—is what the therapeutic process is all about. And it goes on twenty-four hours a day, every moment. I was continually being "pulled up" for being "out of touch" in seemingly trivial but revealing ways, such as seeking a job assignment working on the baseball diamond, where there was minimal social contact, instead of in the kitchen or on the service crew, where you are constantly under the pressure of social exposure. All my instincts toward being a "loner," a lifelong load of them, were constantly probed and questioned, in groups and out. Like most new people in the house, I didn't find it hard to accept criticism, to stay on the defensive. What was hardest for me was to make a pull-up myself in morning meeting, to put myself on the line and question others, as they questioned me. Despite the enormous difference in consequences, the urge to shoot dope and the urge to lie back and play the role in life of the passive observer come from the same place.

There is something of the addict in most of us, but we don't go all the way, as does the junkie. We are running scared, but our softer, more cautious forms of anesthesia—alcohol, pot, sleeping pills, tranquilizers—have a built-in margin of safety. They take the edge off our pain momentarily, but we struggle on, clinging to that margin of safety, for without it, we should have to admit what every junkie does in a community like Daytop: that we have to change, open up to ourselves and to each other, whatever the risks, for without this surrender of our old defenses and reflexes, nothing but a life of evasion, resignation, and compromise is possible. If the junkie out on the street, in his fierce and desperate isolation, epitomizes something of the modern condition of which we are all a part, what then of the ex-junkies, not those tamed off the streets by daily injections of methadone, but those who, through no miracle but a profoundly simple yet difficult process known as the Concept, have come to gain not only freedom from drugs, but self-knowledge, honesty, compassion—in a word, their own essential humanity? What manner of men are they? The answer, I think, is difficult to take. We don't want to believe there really *is* a cure, not just for heroin addiction, but for the whole emotional plague of man which Wilhelm Reich characterized as being "human *evasiveness* with regard to living Life." It is no less a task than this which Daytop, and other communities like it, are engaged in, and, if these most lost souls of our society have found a grace, a salvation, free of all sentimentality, mysticism, and religiosity, rooted only in the joyous acceptance and spontaneity of their own humanity, where does that leave us? Can we take it? As one honest soul, a *Village Voice* reporter named Vivian Gornick, describing her own reactions to the Daytop play called *The Concept*, put it: "Throughout I remained calm, though intensely held. However, at the end of the play, the actors turned toward the audience and one by one each said, 'Will you love me? Will *you* love me?' They came down off the stage and approached members of the audience, their arms outstretched: '*Will* you love me? Will *you* love me?' Suddenly I experienced a moment of terror so pure and so potent that before I knew it I had pressed the arm of my companion and said reassuringly, 'Don't panic. They can't reach the balcony.'" *

That balcony is where most of us are. Perhaps we can still be reached. For our need certainly is as urgent as theirs. And this they know. But let them speak for themselves.

GROVER AMEN

* Reprinted by permission of *The Village Voice*. Copyright by The Village Voice, Inc., 1970.

Greg

GREG WAS BORN IN 1943 and raised in the Italian section of South Boston. It was a tough, old neighborhood frequented by gamblers and a colorful assortment of small-time criminals and Mafiosi, but Greg's parents were well off and had a good house with all the middle class amenities. His mother was a housewife and his father was a construction foreman. He had one sister five years older.

"From the start I was always fighting," said Greg. "I was fast with my hands, even when I was eight and nine. But I had this other soft, sensitive side to me that gave me a lot of trouble, maybe because I was ashamed of it and felt it was a weakness. I was scared to sleep alone, and until I was ten I used to sleep a lot in my sister's bed. But my parents put a stop to that by the time my sister was fifteen. This big, nice idea was built up that I'd be independent and have my own room with horses and cowboys painted on the walls, but I was still scared being alone and I'd ask to have the light left on at night. When I got to sleep, though, my mother would come in and turn the light off and I'd wake up later very frightened and run into my parents' bed. The fear always made me ashamed. I slept between them,

1

and I know now that it was my own imagination, a projection of my sexual fears, but I had the idea that my father was trying to get at me sexually, and I'd run out of the bed. I always had a sexual guilt and fear about my father and, later, I was scared he'd catch me masturbating, which he did one day when I was thirteen. I was in the bathroom with the door latched and was about to reach a climax when my father started beating on the door. When he pushed it open and saw what I was doing, he mumbled something in disgust and looked at me as though I were some kind of weird creep. Then he just walked away, but he left me feeling dirty and perverted."

As a kid, Greg was very athletic. He was a good boxer and won a trophy when he was ten. He was good at football, too, being big and well-built for his age, and by the time he reached junior high he had a clique of boys that hung around him and looked up to him. "I loved that feeling of being admired as a tough guy and a leader. The sense of power—it's beautiful, man. It was like I was king of that school. But I often needed to be alone and I'd disappear for days at a time, like a mysterious criminal lying low. Then I'd surface again with a bang, glorying in my return from exile. I had a great time acting out, and it wasn't fantasy. I always had money, even before I began operating in a big way."

Although Greg was aggressive in sports, he was experiencing considerable turmoil over sex at the age of thirteen. One night he was in his parents' bed again, and this time he was sure that his father was trying to molest him sexually. He became hysterical with fear and ran from the bed. "After that, I started to shy away from everyone in the family," said Greg. "I wouldn't even go over to visit my aunt or my grandmother. I resented my father, and one reason was that everybody thought he was such a great guy. I went along, pretending that I felt the same way. But I really felt that, deep down, he was a phony. And, of course, I was jealous of him. When I walked down the street, the respectable neighborhood people just thought of me as his kid. He got a lot of respect from them because of the things he could do. As a general construction foreman, he could build bridges, pour concrete, do masonry, lay steel, put in heating

2

systems, lay down electrical lines. He could do almost anything with his hands and do it well."

The summer that Greg was fourteen he went up to Boy Scout camp in the country. "While I was up there," said Greg, "I had this other kid go down on me, and eventually the kid squealed, and I was thrown out of camp. My father, who was a scoutmaster, got thrown out too. After that, I started getting into all kinds of small trouble, nothing too serious, vandalism, breaking into vending machines, stealing coins, and I'd often end up in family court. One night I was lying in bed and I heard my father talking about me to my mother. She was trying to defend me, and he was saying, 'Sorry. I don't want any part of that kid. He's no good.' It came to a head one day when I had this baby chicken I'd shot for the hell of it with a BB gun. I was down in the cellar, trying to take the BB out of the chicken, when my father came down the stairs, looked around, and this expression of absolute contempt came over him when he saw what I was doing—involved with this wounded chicken, fiddling with it—and he said to me, 'You sick motherfucker, just what are you trying to do?' "

Greg soon started going his own way completely. He was close-mouthed at home, especially during meals, and he got a kick out of going to the corner store where all the bookies hung out. "They liked me," said Greg. "They'd give me small change to play the jukebox with or set me up on a stool so that I could play the pinball machine. I was less into sports now and was looking elsewhere for my own identity. I used to watch the guys in the store throwing dice, and they got a kick out of me. I was a likable kid, dark, with curly hair and a lot of cheek, and sometimes they'd ask me to roll the dice for them. They'd shout, 'Hey, Greg. I need some luck. Roll for me, will you?' They thought I was lucky. And if I made a couple of numbers for them, they'd give me a few dollars."

Greg became friends with a bookie, a man named John, who was thirty-two. John had a ranch wagon, and one night he gave Greg and another friend, Richie, a tip about a jewelry store where the burglar alarm was out of order. Using John's ranch wagon, Richie and Greg broke into the store and cleaned the entire place out. "The cabinets were full of watches and bracelets, lighters, diamond rings and rubies," said Greg. "We half-filled a potato sack from the stuff in that store—close to $10,000 worth. We were supposed to give it all to John to sell, but he had only cut us in for $500 each on the job, so I held onto some of the stuff myself. Quite a bit, in fact. Then Richie and I went down to New York to celebrate our first big job. We drank a lot and experimented with drugs, nothing hard, just some pills and cough medicine. But I only stayed a few days. I had to come back to appear in court on an old charge. It went back to an incident in a movie theater where I'd busted an usher in the mouth.

"My mother and father came to court with me, and what saved the day was this veterans' Boy Scout pin my father was wearing. Luckily, the judge was wearing one just like it, so with this bond between them, the judge dropped the case and put me on probation."

At the junior high school Greg went to, he had things pretty good, and was looked up to as king of the school. As a sign of their esteem the other kids used to give him their milk at lunch. "I used to drink so much milk at lunch," said Greg, "I'd have the runs all afternoon. The teachers, though, had no use for me. I was like Public Enemy Number One. I especially had trouble with this gym teacher, Mr. Bigelow. Just before gym class one day I was climbing up the ropes and swinging around, like a gorilla. He told me to cut it out. He was a great big guy, but I kept defying him. When class began, we got to playing dodge ball, and I set it up so that the kids were hurling the ball at him. He got so angry that he blew his cool, collapsed, and grabbed his chest like he might be having a heart attack. Someone ran out and got help. Mr. Bigelow was all right, but, when he came around, he said that it was either him or me in that school, so I got thrown out."

At the new junior high Greg was sent to, the ringleader of the school was named George. Greg made friends with him and started to date his kid sister. When George was thrown out and sent to reform school, Greg took his place. "I had the same kind of power as at the first school, maybe more," said Greg.

4

"I wouldn't take the slightest crap from anybody. One day, for instance, two kids bumped into me by mistake, knocking my books down. Without even thinking, I proceeded to beat the shit out of them, kicking one of them in the face over and over while I yelled at him, 'Just who the hell do you think you are?' I kicked him so hard in the head he had a concussion."

That incident resulted in Greg's being transferred to a third junior high, a Catholic school, where there was a very rigid regime presided over by a tough Italian principal. "He was a very dedicated, hard-working type," said Greg, "and just the fact of my existence seemed to outrage him. I had plenty of money. I still had jewelry left from the big haul, and I'd bring it to school and sell it to the other kids. They really dug the fact that the stuff was hot. I made money shooting craps, and I also had a $25 a week allowance from my mother. Because my father and I didn't get along, she liked to indulge me. Anyway, I used to come to school in hundred-dollar suits. It was crazy. I had this black cashmere overcoat I'd wear with a white scarf. I saw myself as a real teen-age Mafioso. I had two steady girl friends at that school, and a third at the old school. I had so much money that I often drove to school in a taxi, which really bugged the principal. He'd say, 'Where do you get these clothes? How do you get the money?' I wouldn't even answer him. I'd just glance at him scornfully, like he was some kind of dirt. One day I ran into him in the hallway. He said, 'What are you doing here?' I said, 'I'm just going to school.' I hadn't done anything wrong, but he said to me, 'Look. I'm not throwing you out. I just don't want you here today. You can go home.' Then he worked his way behind me, scuffing the soles of his shoes against my trouser cuffs. In return, I threw my lunch bag at him and left."

That year Greg played football for the neighborhood league, and the principal tried to reach him through athletics. He asked Greg to play ball for the school, implying that such cooperation might be weighed favorably against his bad record. But Greg turned him down, and, soon after, was transferred back to the first school on probation. There he did get back to athletics, managed to settle down, and that year his team won the football

5

championship. He was a leading player. He kept his grades high and, according to an agreement he had made with the principal, he made up the work he was behind by the end of the school year. This meant that he could start regular high school the next fall.

"But high school was a big blow to my image," said Greg. "In junior high I'd been kingpin, but starting out in high school with all these older guys I felt like a real ding-a-ling. Everybody was bigger than me, and the older girls weren't impressed by my appearance or reputation. I decided to try wrestling. Whenever I used to get beaten, I was very aggressive. I'd go back and try again. But this day I wrestled with an older guy who beat me eight points to seven. For some reason, I lost heart. It wasn't like me, but I didn't care. It worked out that I was sick. A few days later I was running a temperature of 105 degrees; I had spinal encephalitis. There was an epidemic; I heard that people were dying of it all around me. Then I went into a coma, and when I came out of it, I could hardly move. I was laid up for weeks. The encephalitis was followed by pneumonia and measles—all in a period of three months. It was pretty bad and turned all my feelings around. I stayed home, just laying up, waiting to get back into the swing of things. But when I did, I felt strange and weak. I couldn't play ball right. I felt out of it and didn't give a fuck about anything. My mother helped me get a note from the doctor, pulling me out of school. I never went back."

Greg was fifteen when he dropped out of school. Once that step had been taken—a step he could blame, with some justification, on his illness—he made a more conscious effort to establish connections with the gamblers and other underworld-oriented characters in his neighborhood. He had always been attracted to such types, and feeling as he did that his father despised him, it was a satisfying form of revenge to look down on his father and dismiss him as a square. Greg secretly envied the few kids in his neighborhood whose fathers had positions within the syndicate. At this point, his ambition was eventually to make it in the underworld, one way or another, not to drown out any negative feelings he had by getting high on drugs. Already he was aware that pot-heads and junkies were anathema to any but the lowest underworld circles. In fact, Greg didn't fool around much with pot, and he never got hooked—not on heroin. As for cough medicine and pills, that all seemed like a harmless diversion, in the same class as alcohol. He'd been experimenting with cough medicine ever since he was thirteen.

In any case, he began hanging out on the corner, ingratiating himself with older men—pool sharks, small fry with dubious Mafia connections. Because of his age and inexperience, he felt the best way to impress them was by showing skill and speed with his fists. He would pick fights with men bigger than he and usually beat them. He got in a brawl with a waiter in a nightclub and was arrested, but later released. This physical exhibitionism did not produce any immediate job offers from the syndicate. But his older friends would drive Greg around in their cars—and they encouraged him to pop pills. "The first time I was given a couple of yellow jackets—that's Nembutal— I just fell asleep," said Greg. "I didn't like the feeling. But I'd get prescriptions from an old shyster doctor for Nembutals and Dexadrines. Then I went to the family doctor—the same one that had helped pull me out of school—and he gave me another prescription for fifty Nembutals. I didn't take the Nembutals myself—not then. I'd sell them or give them away. They represented more my ability to tap resources—to contribute something of my own to the general lunacy. People could always count on me for a few yellow jackets in a pinch. What insanity! Anyway, I liked the feeling from cough medicine better. What I dug most was this stuff called Cosanyl. It had codeine in it then, and you could get a really powerful high out of it. And you didn't need a prescription. You just had to sign for it, like you do for paregoric in some states. Everybody was buying it— and not for coughs—so the FDA cracked down. You can still get Cosanyl but not with codeine in it. I had this friend who used to drink Cosanyl all day long. He was so hung up on it that he tried to freeze it into ice cubes. 'You and I,' he told me one day, 'we're going into business selling Cocycles.' The trouble was that it wouldn't freeze because of the alcohol in it. He loved to drive around high and toss the empty Cosanyl

7

bottles out the car window. Talked to himself all the time. When I'd ask him why, he'd say, 'That way I always get the right answer.' A real nut!"

When Greg was sixteen, he joined the National Guard, mainly to follow the example set by some of his older friends and also because he was at loose ends. To get accepted, he'd lied about his age, and when, after a few weeks, he got sick of the routine, he got out simply by confessing to his real age. He received a minority discharge.

After getting home, he resolved to make some real gambling contacts. He became adept at shooting craps and would practice at home for hours, plunking dice. "My specialty was making tens and fours," said Greg. "And at last some of the gamblers began to take notice of me. I hung out at this nightclub where the professional boosters drank. They'd give me tips on the trade. Boosters are shoplifters. It was only a misdemeanor as long as you didn't steal more than $150 worth of merchandise from one store. It was easy pickings, and I specialized in records. If you tore the cellophane off the album, once you were out of the store, they couldn't even charge you with theft. The boosters I met had lived and worked all over the country. A good one can easily earn $300 a day, just working three or four hours. The trick is to keep moving. You get to know the country pretty well too.

"Once my friends and I got into boosting, we showed an enormous amount of balls, stealing all the stuff that we did. I was caught a couple of times, but I had so much composure, I could talk my way out of anything. The boosters were smart. They just plied their trade and didn't succumb to grandiose schemes for great bank robberies. We didn't either, but we did get beyond shoplifting. When I got my driver's license, I'd drive the older guys around on their jobs, and they'd give me tips on stuff stored away in warehouses or in railway express stations. We'd often make as much as $500 a night for twenty minutes' work. Liquor was lucrative, as well as hardware, especially television sets. We had our own fences, and that side of the business always ran smoothly. I kept on being a winner when I gambled, and I usually had at least $300 or $400 in my

8

pocket. There were other rackets too we cashed in on, like accident front money. That's where you set up phony automobile accidents that the insurance companies have to pay off on. The money just kept rolling in, and I didn't know what fear was. That's how it was when I was sixteen.

"I was aware of heroin at this time, and I'd shot it a few times, just for kicks, but I wasn't addicted. I shot morphine too, and enjoyed it, but it wasn't the main thing. I was too busy making money. And I was getting more and more brazen. One night I was with two other guys in the railroad yards. It was in an isolated section of the city, and we were trying to take off a whole freight car full of television sets. We had a station wagon, and I was in the front seat, piling up the TV sets in back, when we heard some shots. The other kids made a run for it and got away, but I lost a few seconds by being stuck in the car and I ended up trapped against a brick wall by the night watchman. I thought it was funny because he was more scared than I was. He yelled at me, 'Lie down on your belly.' And I yelled back, 'Go fuck yourself.' I thought I'd get out of it somehow, because it was a real deserted area, and this guy was trembling all over, holding the gun on me. But he got lucky. A car went by, and he fired two shots in the air; the car stopped, and the watchman told them to call the police. Next thing I knew, police cars were all around me, and two of the cops called me by name. I still wasn't scared. I fed them a real line. I told them I was driving by, when two guys stopped me, at gunpoint, insisted that I pull into the freight yard, and began to load TV sets into my car. They took me to the station house and when they asked me how come my fingerprints were on the TV sets, I explained that, as the burglars pushed the sets into the car, I was trying to push them out. Of course the cops didn't buy a word of it, and when I stuck with the story, they proceeded to beat the shit out of me. They were choking me, belting me in the face and stomach, and demanding to know the guys I was working with. I wouldn't talk and the best charge they could hope to make stick was receiving stolen goods. They questioned me for the next seventy-two hours. Because the interstate seal on the freight car had been broken, the federal agents were also called into the case. The feds don't beat you. They let the local cops do the dirty work, and they just move in real quiet and cool and ask you questions. I played stupid, like I didn't know what it was all about. I walked around the room crazy, catching flies with my fist. But the feds picked up on the needle marks on my arm and called me a junkie. After three days of busting my balls, they hadn't gotten me to talk, and they had to let me go on $500 bail.

"When I was released, the fact that I hadn't ratted on anyone gave my reputation a big boost. It helped my own morale too. It was a beautiful feeling to walk into a nightclub with all the big-shots there knowing you'd taken three days of having your balls busted without breaking down. I'd set up drinks for the whole bar, and I began going out with the older hookers that worked in the clubs. I picked up with this beautiful blonde who was twenty-eight, and I became her old man. I was faster than ever with my hands, and all the guys were scared to hassle with me. I was making money hand over fist. I'd give a band five dollars just to play one song. But a subtle change for the worse had taken place since my arrest. I was taking barbiturates more frequently. And now I enjoyed it, whereas before I'd done it socially, to boost my public image, to go along with the crowd. I was operating at such an accelerated pace I needed something to slow me down. Soon I was taking eighteen or twenty Nembutals a day to stay calm, plus amphetamines to give me a lift when I got drowsy or depressed. It got so bad I went to a hospital for eleven days to get detoxified. While kicking, I had muscle spasms and convulsions, and I vowed I'd never swallow another pill.

"Once out, though, I only went one day without drugs. The guys I was stealing with began to pick up on it. Even the pool sharks and gamblers began pushing me away—they didn't want to count on anyone mixed up with dope.

"Worse, I began to lose heart for stealing. I kept on with it, but there was a fear in me now, and sometimes I was high for twenty-four hours a day, only going out for a few hours at night. I began to get very paranoid about small things, like what some guy at a cigar store really thought of me. An older guy,

10

who I liked, warned me, 'Cut out the pills or you're finished.' I kept trying to get myself together, but I was very weak emotionally. I didn't feel I had the guts—in the way I did before, when I was on top. I was also taking morphine, heroin, Dilaudid, and Demerol in addition to Nembutals, Seconals, and every kind of amphetamine. Whenever I stole now I was afraid, which was the reason I kept taking drugs. I know now that being caught that time in the railroad yards had a lot to do with it. That experience represented my loss of innocence. I blamed the fear on the effect of the drugs, but still I couldn't stop taking them."

It was during this period—Greg was now nineteen—that he met his future wife, Diane. She'd had an illegitimate child by another man who'd walked out on her, and she tended to look at Greg as a kind of knight in shining armor. In turn, he looked at her as a fast kid with a car, who'd drive him around, give him money, and help him to get pills. When she got pregnant by Greg, he agreed to marry her, but more as a chivalrous gesture than as an act of conviction. He even used the wedding itself as a means of getting extra drugs. On the way to the justice of the peace, he had her stop at a drugstore to purchase some Cosanyl. She signed for it under her maiden name. On the way back, they stopped there again, and she got a second bottle by signing her married name. "That night in bed with her," said Greg, "I was so fouled up I couldn't get an erection, and I had this disgusted feeling, like I didn't give a damn for her, not really.

"It was horrible. We were living with my parents. I don't know why they put up with it except that they were scared of me and hoped the marriage would straighten me out. I was high all the time now. I was using drugs to block out all the scared feelings I had—that the marriage was a mistake, an accident, and that my wife was beginning to see me for what I was—a pill-head. It got crazy. I fell asleep with a lighted cigarette in my hand one night, and I felt my wife tugging at me saying, 'Get up! The mattress is on fire.' But I didn't care. I rolled over a few inches and told her to mind her own business, and I went back to sleep. My wife kept saying she loved me, and she got

11

me to a sanatorium for a week. As soon as I got out, I went back on drugs. My wife was trying to reform me, and I must have hated her for that. But I don't know. Even hating's a kind of responsibility, and I loved the feeling of not being involved at all. I wanted to do nothing, but I still needed money. Instead of stealing with caution, I began to do crazy things. One day I tried to cash this bum check in a supermarket. I thought my old charisma would see me through. I was starting to believe in magic. The clerk took it to the manager, and he came back to me very politely, as though it might not be my fault, and said, 'Did you know this check was stolen?' Instead of trying to talk my way out of it, I turned chicken and ran out the door like a slob. Five cops grabbed me before I was halfway down the block. They saw I was fouled up with drugs, so first they sent me to the state hospital. Then I returned to the Boston jail, where my parents bailed me out. On my release, the Marblehead police picked me up and put me in a line-up involving some burglary. Nobody there identified me, so I was freed. But an attorney general told me, 'Sooner or later you're going to jail for good.' And I was scared.

"I decided it was time to reform. I was nineteen. I went to work for my father, after convincing him that I was sincere about turning over a new leaf. My wife was working, and we had enough money to get our own apartment and buy some furniture. Getting back in a work routine made me feel almost normal, and I decided I didn't need pills any more—that I'd just been acting out against some old pain and that now everything was going to be all right. The baby was coming soon, a kind of peace came over me, and I felt I was starting to fall in love with my wife.

"The baby came, and we were pretty happy. We had our own place, new furniture, and I felt secure. I was working. Diane was getting unemployment insurance. It was almost as much as she'd made when she was working. We were building a life of our own. I was off drugs and pills. I was drinking, but very lightly. I'd just go and have a few beers after work with my father or some of the other guys on the job. There was no real problem until winter set in and I got laid off work. Once

12

that happened, my wife took the attitude that I should go out and get another job. By that time she was working again and we'd gotten a baby-sitter. Her mother, too, was baby-sitting for a while. But what happened was that when I became idle, I began to drink to excess. It got to the point that my wife said, if I was going to stay home, I ought to take care of the baby and save the baby-sitting money. I didn't want to do that. I was drinking more. My nerves were on edge, and I couldn't face the stress and strain I'd have to go through, taking care of the baby by myself. I tried it for a few days, but I was doing all kinds of crazy shit, man. I would leave the baby in the morning after my wife had gone to work, when I knew I shouldn't, and run down to the liquor store and bring home a bottle. I'd drink and fall asleep, then give the baby its bottle and change the diapers. I'd always make sure that the house was cleaned up by the time my wife got home. But it was all very sneaky and dope-fiendish, and I was really starting to get turned off from myself. I felt I was doing her job, and she was constantly hollering and bickering at me about why I wasn't out looking for a job. I'd always been very aggressive and demanding of my wife, but all of a sudden there was this turn-around. It was like I was falling in love with her, and she was placing demands on me. It was quite a change, and I didn't like it one goddamn bit. Whereas I was always the one in control before our marriage and up until the baby came, now she was in control, and slowly but surely I started to regress. Another thing: I'd put on twenty to thirty pounds, and it had gotten to a point that I'd turn her off so much, she no longer even wanted to go to bed with me. I can remember one horrible night, when I was in bed with her, getting up in the middle of the night and thinking I was in the bathroom, and urinating all over her. Like it's funny now, but at the time it was disgusting. She told me that she was fed up and was going to quit her job. I was still getting $48 a week in unemployment, but I used to drink most of it up, and I started going back to my old neighborhood on weekends, hanging out with the guys. I was looking for a place to fit in again because I'd pushed myself out of my own house. My wife was assuming the male posture. And I was playing her role, or that's the way

13

I felt, anyway. I got high in the old neighborhood, and when I got home she picked up on it, and the shit really began to hit the fan. Finally, I got to the point where I was feeling so screwed up about me, because of what I had let happen, her controlling the house and the money, that I reverted back to my old street bag and became nasty and arrogant and told her I didn't need her and to go fuck herself. I said I wanted no more part of the whole scene. I left and when I came back, she was gone. Two days later she returned and wanted to know what I was going to do. I told her, 'I think the best thing is that we separate. I don't want to be married any more.' She wanted me to stay and get a job and try to make things work, but I'd reached a point where I didn't want to hear another word. I just wanted to go out and get high. I walked out on her.

"There were things that contributed to me getting back to that point. One was this kid my wife had by another guy. It began to bug me after we got married. And my mother-in-law was over at my house eight nights a week, man, and was bringing that kid over and intruding into everything. When I saw that kid, my belly would flip. I couldn't really accept it. Whenever it was around, I felt like banging it in the head. My wife never asked me if he could live with us. I might have said yes, and then taken all my shit out on him. I don't know. Anyway, it got me when my mother-in-law came over with him. At first I just sat in my chair and watched television and drank beer and ignored them; then it got to the point where I couldn't stand it. My parents moved, but I didn't want to go to the new neighborhood with them. Instead, I went back to the old neighborhood, and I hooked up with this kid named Allen. He was married and had kids and his own place, and I started staying with him, and we worked together well, stealing. We made a few small scores, $90 apiece, and he didn't cheat me. If he made a score, and I happened to be with him, he'd give me half of it, and I got to like him because of that. We had a trust and became close friends. He wouldn't beat me out of anything, and I wouldn't beat him, not in the beginning anyway. We started hustling and stealing and made some serious money. One time we took off this place and wound up making $1,000 apiece.

14

We were going to nightclubs again, balling chicks, and I felt good. It's a funny thing, whenever I've got money, money's like dope to me. When I've got big money, I don't use drugs, or I use them very lightly. I'd rather go out and wine and dine. I don't even drink that much. Big money is like pure power to me. . . .

"At the same time I'd been going through a lot of pain. People think that when you're on dope you just blot everything out, but it's not true. You can blot it out when you're high, maybe right after you've shot stuff or taken some pills, but it doesn't last, and the pain is always there. And it's not always the pain that gets you; it can be the healthier, outgoing emotions you don't want to feel either. Some of the feelings, oddly enough, that I was trying to get away from were feelings of compassion for other people. One part of me had always been concerned with reaching out toward other people, but whenever I did, it seemed to backfire. I was oversensitive. I remember, for instance, one Palm Sunday giving my sister a beautiful palm leaf and a cake. She just set the palm leaf aside, as though it were nothing, and when she sliced the cake open, she said, 'What's this? It's nothing but frosting.' I felt like she'd stuck the knife into me. And I took a pledge to destroy all those outgoing feelings. I knew that I always felt a lot but that people seemed to push me away. At first I withdrew, but then I stopped withdrawing and became arrogant. When you get tired of being hurt and withdrawn, you want to hurt back and strike out.

"A few months after leaving my wife, I was in a bar and met this broad named Louise. She was without doubt the most repulsive person I ever met in my entire life. She was four feet ten inches high and weighed 190 pounds. I began living with her. She had these five dirty kids and lived in this repulsive apartment absolutely stinking with dirt and grime and garbage and stray food. It's even hard for me to explain or rationalize, whatever my condition was then, how I ended up with her except for wanting to debase and humiliate myself as much as possible. Bottles lay all over the floor and were never picked up. I was a hired stud. I banged her. In return she let me have a roof over my head and I could share her welfare check, which came to $105 every two weeks. This was the lowest point in my life. At the same time a friend of mine who'd robbed a drug wholesaler gave me 15,000 barbiturate pills. Now, in anybody's book, that's quite a supply of pills. It meant that I had an apparently inexhaustible supply for my own needs, and whenever I needed money for liquor or stronger stuff, I could just go out and sell some of my pills. So, for the time being, even the incentive toward crime was removed, not that I had any taste for it anyway. I'd become a total vegetable and coward, and at this point I was completely hooked on pills, not on heroin. Most people think that a heroin habit is the worst thing that there is; but it's not true. A real barbiturate habit is worse. Of course I'm not talking about taking a few pills at night. When I was hooked on Nembutals, I was taking twenty-five or thirty a day, at least two every couple of hours. When you take that many, it gets harder and harder to reach that drowsy high, and, when you're coming down, the psychological symptoms are worse than heroin withdrawal. When you're not on the verge of absolute panic, you're completely paranoid and confused. You can't control your muscular movements, and sometimes you literally can't talk straight. You talk backward, making no sense, and then you get into a rage of impotence when people don't understand you. In effect, you become a blithering idiot. In the ranks of dope addicts, pill-heads rank on the very lowest echelons.

"But to get back to the house, there was hardly any heat in it all winter. I never washed my clothes. Louise never washed her clothes or any of the kids' clothes. She was an absolute douche bag. I didn't always stay there. It was more like a dog house I could crawl in and out of, according to my mood. And I hated it so much that a lot of times I slept in doorways rather than crawl into bed with her. Sometimes, in fact, I wouldn't go to bed for days. Instead of sleeping for eight hours a third of each day, I'd stay up, dozing off for twenty minutes or so wherever I was, sitting on a stoop or on a bar stool. It was a sleeping pattern that fitted in better with the barbiturate habit. I looked so repulsive that people would turn away or cross the street if they saw me coming. On my twentieth birthday—I felt

16

so lonely and fucked up that I picked a fight with a total stranger and tried to stab him. But my speed and coordination were so bad that I just got beaten up. I began shaking people down on the street, threatening them if they wouldn't give me a few coins. The only social activity I was capable of was going out to the racetrack and betting on the horses; I wasn't up to that very often. I wasn't even up to getting involved in a crap game. The sheer physical exertion of rolling dice seemed too much for me, and the mathematics too much for my confused head. But I still had my reservoir of pills. And Louise would give me spending money now and then. Very occasionally, after getting high on heroin, I'd pull off a small burglary with Allen, but he did most of the work. I was just there, trying to prove that I still had balls. After one of these Mickey Mouse-type operations, Allen got busted. We had an agreement. I should have gone down and at least tried to scare the money up to bail him out. But I didn't do anything. I didn't even try. I think I was probably relieved he'd gotten busted. My relationship with him was one more responsibility I didn't have to worry about. I began pimping in a bar for a black broad I knew.

"The only good thing that happened during this year was my meeting this girl named Debbie. I met her through a friend named Jim that I went to stay with. He was a nice guy from the old days. When he saw the shape I was in, he invited me to stay with him and get straightened out. I didn't try to kick the barbiturate habit, but I did manage to cut down enough so that I was rational and hopeful. Just getting out of Louise's house was terrific. Living with her was equivalent to total dissipation and self-destruction. At Jim's I began to eat better, to shave, and to wear clean clothes. And I was able to talk to him about how fucked up everything had gotten. Above Jim lived this girl named Debbie who had two kids. One night I got high on heroin which gave me the courage to approach her. I went up, announced myself, saying I was a friend of the fellow downstairs, and she invited me in. I felt good. It seemed like years since I'd just sat around with a normal girl as though I were a normal man. I was full of social self-confidence, telling stories, being a real charmer, and suddenly I threw out the question,

17

'Hey, by the way, if you feel like getting laid, let me know, because that would be real nice.' It seemed like a natural thing to come out with, and she said, 'No. I've only just met you.' But we went on rapping and having a good time. After another hour or so, I wasn't in the mood for sex at all. I wasn't even sure I'd be able to get it up. I was just happy at having met her and I didn't want my proposition put to the test then, so I tried to make a graceful exit. I said, 'I think it's time I went downstairs.' But she said, 'No, no. Please stay.' I was really on the spot. I felt that my manhood was at stake. I did stay, and it eventually worked out all right. From then on, I had a nice relationship with her. She always had food in the house. She treated her kids real nice, and she made me feel at ease with them. I felt that Debbie was my only link with normality and real life. But Debbie didn't even know I took drugs. And I didn't want her kind of life enough to level with her and admit everything, so the relationship was doomed."

One night Greg tried to rob a doctor's office. In the process of kicking open the medicine cabinet, he cut his foot on the glass door. His foot was bleeding so badly that he had to hail a cab and head for the emergency room of the nearest hospital. Once there, however, his concern shifted from his bleeding foot back to getting drugs, and he managed to divert the attention of the doctor and nurses just long enough to pocket some liquid cocaine, some morphine, and a handful of sleeping pills. Since this was the first instance in some time that Greg had showed any of his old daredevil spirit, he took considerable pleasure in narrating the episode to Jim and a few other friends. The trouble was that the story quickly got to Debbie, who did not find it funny. She had a serious talk with Greg—during which he admitted how strung-out he was on pills—and she told him: "It's no fucking good, Greg. I don't want to see you any more, until you get straightened out."

"Instead of trying to straighten out," says Greg, "I only took the incident as a way of confirming that I wasn't worthy or capable of having any relationship with a normal girl."

He went back to Louise: "I went back to her with the feeling that I was going to end my days there. There seemed nothing

18

to look forward to. A bunch of other people, so-called friends, began hanging out there too. We just laid up there and drank and took pills. We tossed the empty bottles on the floor, we yelled and cursed at the poor fucking kids, we played records all night. We just indulged in absolute slobbery of every form, and the more destructive it was, the better. It was so repulsive, and there were so many complaints in the neighborhood, which we relished and defied, that we were eventually evicted by court order. I'm not exaggerating: the day we left, people were lined up on both sides of the street, cheering and clapping. We enjoyed that too.

"The new house we moved to didn't have enough heat. The furnace was always going off too soon, so one night I got pissed off and I went down and put some bubble gum on the reset switch to keep it open—so it couldn't cut off. About six hours later the whole furnace exploded and went up in flames. The firemen came and kept the house from burning down, but it meant there was no heat at all for the rest of that winter. We were all freezing to death, trying to stay warm next to the oven and using little electric coil heaters. I caught pneumonia and went to the hospital. While I was there, I couldn't get pills, and I went through convulsions and hallucinations. Again I vowed to myself to stop drugs when I got out. But it meant nothing. It was too easy to take pills, and I still had a lot of that huge supply left.

"Sometimes I would run into my wife. She would drive me around in her car, and we'd talk. It wasn't unfriendly, but I always had this urge to do something completely perverse to hurt her. One time we were having a perfectly civilized conversation and I suddenly decided out of the blue to tell her that I was living with the most repulsive girl in existence and that I wanted my wife to meet her, just so she'd know once and for all where things were at. To show her what I'd become. My wife thought it was some kind of joke. She came along with me back to the house, more or less to humor my whim, and there was Louise in bed, in the middle of the afternoon, with gnawed chicken bones all over the sheets, and the kids running around the house filthy and half naked, and I said to my wife, 'I would like you to meet the woman I love.'

"My wife took one look at this whole scene and became hysterical. She left the house in tears. I felt like a complete degenerate, which I was.

"I still had a few friends who would pick me up from time to time and drive me around. I didn't really like even talking to them, but it felt good to get out of the cold for a while. Now dig this. All this was in 1966. About a month ago I went back to Boston to get a kid out of jail and bring him to Daytop; I don't know where she could have heard that I was coming up there, but I walked into the station house and who was there but Louise. I could tell she was waiting for me. She looked exactly the same, fat and sloppy. If anything, she was even fatter. This time I felt more pity for her than hatred, but I didn't feel enough of it to go over and speak to her. She was still to me an absolute degenerate, lying, phony, sneaky, belligerent bitch and sot. As a human being I'd never seen anything so repulsive. When I used to live with her, such moods of rage and frustration would come over me that I longed to torture her to death. If I could have gotten away with it, I would have. And those brats of hers, those kids, were so much like her that I hated them too. Just once they got back at me! I'd lost a bottle of Nembutals. I'd last seen them on the mantelpiece, I thought. There was a hole in the mantelpiece that led down to the furnace. When the kids heards that I'd lost some pills, one of them told me that the bottle had fallen down that hole. I went down to the furnace, where there were ashes and shit two feet deep, and I grubbed around in there for two hours trying to find the pills. One of the kids comes down to the cellar, and he says, 'What are you doing in there, Greg? Your pills are behind the mantelpiece.' I would have torn the kid apart with my bare hands, but he got away. I was so slow and awkward sometimes, from being stupefied on pills, that I felt like a dinosaur or something. Something monstrous and extinct."

Eventually Greg's barbiturate reservoir ran dry. The 15,000 pills had been either stolen, sold, or consumed. "Because of my monstrous apathy," explained Greg, "I was having trouble getting anything to keep my nerves calmed down. I didn't have the balls for stealing any more, and this intolerable sadness, despair, and self-disgust came over me. If I couldn't get pills for the day, I drank cheap wine. But wine didn't do what the pills did. I tried to hustle cash from anyone I met. Most of them turned me down. Eventually I went to my mother. She didn't want to see me. But I thought I could get around her. I begged her to get a prescription from her doctor and give me the pills. She said she wouldn't. I don't know what was in my head. I began to hide across the street from the house and follow her when she went shopping or to see friends. Sometimes I'd stay back, so she couldn't see me. Other times I'd rush up to her and say, 'Have you gotten those pills yet?' She looked so fragile and preoccupied. She'd say, 'No, Greg. Leave me alone.' In contrast to my father, I'd always thought of her as weak and pliable, and it enraged me that she wouldn't do what I said. 'You better get those pills,' I told her. And I showed her the knife I carried around with me. I wasn't exactly threatening her with it, not personally, but I wanted her to know that I had it, and I followed her all the way home. Once she was inside, this police car pulled up. I was always imagining police cars pulling up behind me, so once it happened, I wasn't too surprised. I threw the knife in the bushes. When the cops stopped and got out of the patrol car, instead of leaving the knife alone, I dove into the bushes to get it back. One of the cops said, 'You better slow down.' I just picked up the knife, pointed it toward them, and said, 'Go ahead, you motherfuckers. Go ahead and shoot me. I just don't give a shit.' With that, the cops fired a shot between my legs. This scared the hell out of me. I dropped the knife, and they put handcuffs on me."

When Greg got to court, the judge sent him to the hospital. There they decided that he needed a sedative—Nembutal. But they didn't give him enough. He had been drinking so much that he was on the verge of getting the DT's. He was in a panic and hallucinating. Meanwhile, he was charged with assault with a deadly weapon. They held him several days for observation. When he made bail, they appointed him a public defender, and he got a postponement on condition that he go to a psychiatrist. "That shrink gave me just what I wanted," said Greg. "A prescription for Nembutals and some Librium, a tranquilizer. I doubt if two people in the world ever exchanged more lies and bullshit than I did with that psychiatrist. It was unbelievable. He bought everything I said, and he seemed to understand everything except that I was an addict. It was pathetic. I got as many barbiturates from him as I wanted, but I kept assuring him that I was honestly tapering off. One thing that helped bring this game to a halt was the lawyer the court had appointed me. He started to get angry because I wasn't paying him the money I'd promised him. He told me, 'If you don't get the money up, you can get ten years, and I'll see that you do.'

"More important, I'd been to a social service agency in Boston that was trying to help out drug addicts and delinquents. There was one guy there that I liked very much and he'd taken me one night to meet Father Egan who was known in Massachusetts as the "junkie priest" for his helping of addicts. I was very impressed by what he said. I didn't take it too seriously, but still, it left a kind of hopeful feeling in the back of my mind. Somewhere I'd known all along that things couldn't keep going on like this. That I'd either commit suicide or start some new kind of life. But this was just lazy, wishful thinking. Something had to give somewhere. Maybe if I'd become a successful criminal, things would have been different. But my use of dope had ruined any possibility of that long ago. There just had to be some other place for me to start.

"On the advice of Father Egan and my social-worker friend, I voluntarily committed myself for thirty days to the city hospital. It was like a half jail, half hospital. That's where I ended up on Christmas Eve of 1966. I was put in the ward with the old men and the psychos and the alcoholics. Oddly enough, there were no other addicts there. I guess all but me were smart enough to stay out of that place. I couldn't sleep. I felt that everybody was squatting on me. So I escaped, which wasn't too difficult. I just slipped out in the middle of the night, past a guard. I had an aunt that I liked who I'd kind of been saving for a rainy day. I went to her house for a while, got some money, and then my parents came over and drove me to a hotel room. I didn't know what to do next. There seemed no place to go. I was just sitting in the hotel room, drinking a pint of booze, when two detectives came to the door. After leaving me, my parents had notified the police. They took me away. But instead of putting me back in that city hospital, they took me to the state hospital. I'd thought the first place was bad, but it was like kindergarten compared to the state place. It was a real funny farm. They gave you these uncomfortable pajamas made of something like asbestos. You could smoke one cigarette an hour under supervision. I was really frightened. Most of the people there were crazy, and I felt that I was going crazy too. It was a Stone Age place where they hadn't even heard of using tranquilizers for people who were emotionally disturbed. Luckily, my friend from the social agency came to see me, and promised to help. I was worried about the other two charges hanging over me, one involving the freight car incident and the other my trying to cash the bad check at the supermarket. He confirmed that on the first I'd received six months' probation and that the second, still pending, would probably be dropped since I hadn't actually cashed the check. He also told me about a therapeutic community called Daytop. At that point, with only the assault charge hanging over me, I probably could have gotten out of the whole jam and gone back on the streets. But I was fed up. When he arranged an interview for me at Daytop, I went. That was at the Swan Lake house in February of 1967. When I got there, a girl from my old neighborhood was in the prospect interview for me, and I put on this real tough-guy act. They told me to drop it. It was really scary. They were all screaming at me. There were over two hundred people there then for a retreat. Seeing so many people together scared me. I felt they were all against me.

"I had a very rough time starting at Daytop. I didn't trust anybody. I felt they were talking about me and my inadequacies. I used to sneak up to the bathroom or pick up a newspaper without reading it, just to hide behind it. For two and a half months I didn't smile or laugh, in groups or out. The director-ship saw that I was in pretty bad shape and arranged a meeting for me with Dr. Casriel, the medical superintendent. He prescribed a strong tranquilizer for me, Stelazine, to help get me out of this paranoid state. Now this was strange. Even after this medication was prescribed, something kept me from taking it. I didn't want to be the only person taking medication and I felt like it would postpone what was going to happen inside me, so I never took any of the pills. I kept on feeling bad. One of my feelings was that I felt inadequate as a man, homosexual feelings. It wasn't so much that I had homosexual tendencies, it was more that I felt people thought I was a homosexual. And I couldn't reconcile this with the tough-guy image that I actually did project. At Daytop we learn that almost everyone has homosexual fears. I knew it was all right for other people to have this fear of homosexuality but I didn't feel it was all right for me. Then I had a bad experience. I was rooming with a guy who later became director of the Swan Lake house. One night he folded his pants on a chair and later found seventy-five cents missing. He looked at me accusingly, and I said I didn't take it. I think he believed me. He said so, but word of the incident got around, and the Italian guys in the house that I'd been hanging around with, they came up and kidded me about it, picking up seventy-five cents and then lying. Later on in the night my roommate apologized to me. He'd found the money. It had fallen into the lining of his pocket. Since there was doubt in the house as to whether I'd taken it or not, he was going to make an announcement in the morning meeting to clear it up. But I said, 'No, I want to stand on my own. Tell the coordinators about it. But don't tell the house.' I felt good about doing this. It was the first time I'd withstood public opinion by standing on my own feet. Before that I was always worried about what people thought of me.

"About two and a half months after arriving in Daytop I went into my first marathon. That's a group that lasts from Friday evening until Sunday afternoon, with the emphasis on getting into one's repressed emotions. For the first time I was able to speak about my inadequacies and homosexual feelings. I saw what an enormous weight of self-guilt I'd been carrying and how I'd tended to see myself and all my problems as being unique. But this was unrealistic. Other guys had done worse things, and they were coming out of their guilt and isolation. I felt so much better after that. I got a good mental understanding, but in time the old feelings came back. I wasn't helped by being mixed up with these Italian guys, by still being concerned about what they thought of me. I felt that I shouldn't have to keep all my emotions in for groups and marathons. One of the guys I trusted the most, I talked to him about it one night, about my feeling like a homo, and I expected some sort of a sympathetic response. I felt I was putting myself out on a limb by doing this. But when I told him I felt like a homo, he looked at me and said, 'Well, are you?' This didn't help. It made me feel that all this understanding was a kind of act that people put on within groups because it was expected of them and because that's what groups were for; but that outside of groups people were still their old hostile, suspicious selves, and this made me again distrust people and become paranoid around the house.

"Another thing bothered me: although I'd made some progress up at Swan Lake, they were talking about sending me down to New York on a medical trip—a prospect that terrified me. I was scared of facing people I didn't know at Staten Island, and I told the director, 'If you send me to Staten Island, I'm sure I'll split behind my anxiety.' And each time the date for my medical trip came up, I would somehow manage to get out of it at the last minute. But I reached a point where no further postponements were possible. Everybody was seeing through my subterfuges. Before I went down on the trip, I spoke to the director for about forty minutes. I told him my fears, but he said that I would simply have to deal with them. So off I went to Staten Island in a very negative state of mind.

"It turned out that the fellow I was making the trip with wanted to split too, so shortly after we got to the house at Staten Island, we left together, then took off in different directions. Once I'd made the decision to split, I felt terrible. This is one of the scary and terrible things about splitting after you've been in Daytop awhile. You don't feel the same. You can't hurl yourself into the old escape routes with the same enthusiasm and abandonment as before. It loses its exotic appeal. You're suddenly just out there, and you're scared. You know it's not going to lead anywhere, and you can't kid yourself any more and pretend that you're going to have a great time, that it's going to be a ball. You know deep down inside that you're *not doomed* to be an addict the rest of your life. But this fact is a terrible thing to face up to. It's the beginning of responsibility. And that one word is sheer terror to a guy like me. So I was in a bitch of a state after I split. I wasn't planning on shooting dope. I just wanted to get out of the pressures of Daytop. And the pressures here are terrible for some people. They're tough anyway. There's no getting around it. That's one reason I'm not completely against the methadone program, the way most people in Daytop and the other therapeutic communities are. I feel that some people just can't take this kind of regime. Their nerves may not be up to it. Let's face it. The splittee rates show this. For people who've been in Daytop more than three months, maybe 75 percent of them stay to graduate. But before that, about half the new people split. What's to become of them? There ought to be something in between the therapeutic communities—which really do change you—and ending up shooting dope back on the streets. Maybe the methadone maintenance program is the answer—at least as a last resort. And the pressures in the houses are greater now than when I came in. Guys who split now are very lucky if they even get a chance to come back. There are too many people waiting to get in. There's at least 100,000 addicts out there on the streets of New York, and only room for about 2,000 of them at Daytop, Phoenix, Odyssey, and other smaller houses. With statistics like these, nobody's in the mood to pamper people who want to split. It's rough. But I don't think that when one of us succeeds, we should say, 'This is the only way to do it.' Because I was one of the guys who almost didn't make it."

After splitting, Greg called home to Boston and talked to his sister. He didn't tell her what had happened. He just said that he had permission to come home for the weekend. Then he went to Times Square, bought a bottle of wine, and ended up drinking it alone in a movie. From his own desolation and that of Times Square, a train to Boston seemed the best relief. Waiting at Grand Central, he fell into conversation with a man who had a girl with him. But the man turned out to be a homosexual. He followed Greg out on the street, trying to proposition him. Greg got rid of him and took the train to Boston. There he asked his mother for money. She turned him down and told him the police would be after him if he had quit Daytop. "I didn't know what to do," said Greg. "I went back to Louise and within three minutes we were in bed. But afterward there was nothing for me to say to her, and I didn't feel right there, and I left the house. I picked up again with my old friends including Allen, but I couldn't identify with them. I was between two worlds and I couldn't quite commit myself to either one of them. I was full of fear. I began to steal again. I just couldn't find any feeling of comfortability. I was with Allen one night and he was smacking his girl around and I said, 'For Christ's sake, cut that shit out.' He turned on me and he said, 'Hey what did they do to you in that Daytop place? Turn you into a pussy?' I was scared of getting busted, too, and I knew that was in the cards. Within a week I was back on amphetamines and barbiturates and booze. Two weeks later I was picked up by the police at Louise's place. My family had tipped them off. From the police station I went to court. Leaving Daytop meant I'd violated my parole, so I was put right into the joint. There it was strange. I was rapping with the guys I used to know on the street. They were talking about planning to knife some guy who had been a stool pigeon. All they talked was violence and treachery. I wanted so much to identify with them. I wanted to identify with them more than with Daytop people, but I couldn't. It all seemed degrading to me. I put on a good act outside, but inside I wasn't there at all. I wrote a poem one night:

> It snaps me back to reality, this
> place where they keep society. Shame.
> Crying. Pacing. Living in self-
> degradation. God. The feeling of
> loneliness is everywhere, crawling
> up my spine in the cold night air.
> Seems like I've been here for an

eternity. Please help me. I can't
accept this to be my reality.

"When my friend from the social agency came to see me, we
arranged for a court hearing, and I told the judge I wanted to go
back to Daytop. But I was still screwed up. What I really
wanted was to play it both ways—spend a month or two at Daytop, go back to the street for a while, then back to Daytop. It
was all lunacy. Before going back to Daytop I acted very serious
and said it was important that I see my wife before returning.
I had one thing on my mind. I was full of booze when I went to
see her. I got her into the bedroom and balled her. We had a
few drinks while the Daytop people waited for me outside, and
that was it.

"I got to Daytop at one o'clock and I was put in the prospect
chair. By seven I was ready to split again, it was so bad. Then I
went into the director's office. He smoked the shit out of me. He
said, 'You miserable bastard, go get out there and have your head
shaved.' I wanted to run. I was thinking of being in New York
again, even though I'd just been through all that. The whole
thing of freedom suddenly seemed so beautiful, just to be in a
hotel room in New York, without pressure, without people. But
I stayed. They made me sit in this prospect chair, facing the
wall, hour after hour. I had nothing to eat. Baloney sandwiches
now and then. Every four or five hours I was allowed to smoke
one cigarette. I just sat staring at that wall. I had been in the
prospect chair for fifty-six hours. Up to that point I was withdrawn and passive, and then I became angry and arrogant. This
time it'd been fourteen hours since I'd had anything to eat. One
of the rules of the house is that when somebody's in the prospect
chair you don't speak to him; but one of the older guys came
around to me—he knew what I was going through—and he said,
'Hang tough!' and he went away. Then when I saw the director
come out I said, 'Look, I'm not an animal, I'm human. You can
stuff the whole concept up your ass.' He looked at me and he
said, 'Okay, you can get out of the chair in a while and then we'll
send you home.' Up to this point the director of the house had
acted very hard and rigid to me. All of a sudden he called me

into his office alone and we started rapping. He was very under-standing. I talked about my feelings. He turned them all around for me. I realized I wanted to stay and he said, 'You're going to have an interview first, then a general meeting. You've forgotten everything you learned when you were here. Let's just start from scratch, all right?' I went back to the prospect chair. It was now seventy-two hours I'd been sitting there. I was scared. They said, 'Come on now and be interviewed.' I was hysterical by then. My feelings were beginning to come back to me, but I couldn't quite face them. I began laughing, like a kid. Then I was put before the entire house. People who cared about me began banging away at me, trying to shock me into some kind of real-ity. They tried to show me how dishonest I was being. I still had this resentment about having to be in this humiliating posi-tion at all. They wouldn't let go. They dressed me up, for a learning experience, in diapers. I wasn't allowed to wear any shirt or pants. I had these diapers made out of torn sheets and I was supposed to carry a doll. This was to show me that I was acting like a baby. It made me numb. I had no feelings at all. I was like a gladiator in a lion's den. Another friend of mine said, 'What about those feelings of yours? Those homosexual feelings. How are they?' I said, 'What feelings?' And as soon as I'd said that, denied my feelings, I began to relate to them. A desire to surrender came over me.

"I felt they all expected me to humiliate myself, to show that I was ready to come back again, so I got down on my knees and I begged, 'Please take me back. Take me back into the house. Help me!' A friend of mine yelled at me, 'For God's sake, get up off your knees.' I did, in my diapers, carrying the doll around. I was put in the lowest position in which people start at Daytop, spare parts, shining shoes, the garbage detail.

"All I could think about after the general meeting and the seventy-two hours on the prospect chair was sleep and food. I was willing to accept anything to get that. After a night's sleep, I was told to work in the cesspool and clean out all the shit. That was the major activity of the job entitled 'spare parts.' I worked there for three days, and then I was assigned to rub and polish all the woodwork in the house.

"There was another guy, a big black dude, who'd also been acting out like a baby, and he had to go around with a big red ribbon in his hair. One day the two of us were assigned to carry some pipes out into the woods. I'll never forget this. He wearing the red ribbon and me half naked with my diapers and doll, we were crossing the road when a couple of fishermen saw us. They just looked at us and shook their heads, without even laughing. They must have figured that's what we did for kicks! Even in the house it was especially strange during this period because Daytop was holding groups for outsiders, community people, psychologists and all. So there were squares all over the house pretending not to look at us. Jesus! It was one thing to have residents in the house see you in diapers. They knew what it was all about. But to have these guests glancing away from you as though you were some kind of insane creep—it was rough."

After thirty days Greg slowly emerged from his state of shock. He began to enjoy doing simple physical things in the house. In the kitchen he worked his way up to being ramrod, that is, second in command.

Two weeks later he was made department head of the kitchen. From there he became an expediter, then a project head on maintenance. "I was doing good," he said. "I'd been getting in touch with a lot of my feelings in groups. Especially the shame and disgust and guilt. Those are the most painful feelings to relate to, because there is nothing glamorous about them. But as long as you block them out, they keep eating away at you. Once you admit that's where you're at, you begin to get free. For the first time I began to feel worthy of other people's love. Then I was able to help other people too. Eventually, I became a junior guru, which was the equivalent of a coordinator trainee, dealing with human interaction problems in and out of groups. In other words, if you had problems, I was the first guy you talked to. It was the kind of job I'd always wanted—working with other people. I kept on plugging. I began running probes—they're overnight groups which usually deal with one specific subject, like guilt or fear about homosexuality.

"One of my troubles now was that I tended to throw myself

in an extroverted fashion into these activities, especially in groups, but I failed to relate to my own more sneaky instincts. It was strictly a hangover from the old street days. This came up when I heard that one of the older guys at the house was planning to split. A strict Daytop rule is that when you hear of something like that, you tell about it immediately. It's not like the code of jail and the street where you cover up for people. I don't know why I didn't. But having failed initially, I really got sneaky. I found out that the directorship already knew about it. Only then, to cover up for myself, I went into the director's office and told them what I knew. It was a classic example of sneaky-type manipulation. It's behind guilt over small things like that that people start to feel bad and think about splitting. In any case, the guy did split but came back the next day, when a house meeting was called to deal with him—to find out why he split and how he had told so many people without the directorship being informed sooner. I knew that I was being considered for the position of full guru, but I'd been dishonest, and I finally copped to it, and told everybody exactly what had happened, how sneaky I'd been. This made me relieved inside, but it meant that I was shot down to the service crew.

"This time, though, I had good motivation and drive. Very soon I became department head of maintenance again. And when the next round of job changes came up, I finally landed the position of senior guru. The job had the same status as being a coordinator, and I loved it. I really felt good. I was doing my thing. I was attending staff meetings. I ran a training marathon that was a big success. In it, I got one of the assistant directors to talk about how very rigid and controlled his position made him feel. How he felt he had to block out all his own feelings to keep up his image. This was something I'd been through myself. I was still in it. I'm still in it now. But I was able to help him a lot—to show how being in a position of authority doesn't require playing some rigid paternal role. You'd think people in Daytop would know this instinctively from all they've been through. But it's tricky. It's so much a part of our social conditioning—the idea that you can't quite be yourself when you're on the job—that if you do, you'll give yourself away. Anyway he told me afterward how good I was in this area of groups—that I'd really helped him to see the authority rut he was in. And this is what I want to do in life, even if I don't stay in Daytop— work in some kind of community or group therapy. Anyway, I soon got a new job title—assistant in research and training.

"This was part of a program under the director, David Deitch, in which we were doing a lot of work letting outside people participate in the concept and learn our techniques.

"During this time all the pressures that led to a big split in the house were building up. Some people didn't like David Deitch's political views and thought he had too much power in the directorship, but I didn't take the political aspects of David's position too seriously. I was so busy in groups and so hopeful about what they could do, and David was very much behind me on this. Politics just wasn't my bag, and I only saw him as a guy who believed, as I did, that the kind of work being done in Synanon and Daytop could spread into the outside community and change much that was sick in America. It was obvious that David had a good-sized ego. But it didn't seem likely to me that the board of trustees would fire him. My feeling was that it would all get straightened out eventually if everybody was honest with each other. But soon we got word that some kind of separation was being formulated. I was told to stay upstate in Swan Lake to bolster our strength there. If any sides were to be taken, I was on the David Deitch side then, simply because he was the director. And one night the call came: the split was real. Daytop was in trouble. For me this was bad news —you could also call it the news that the weak side of me was waiting for. There were a few top people in the house who just decided to hang tough and didn't want to split behind this crisis. But for people like me who were still unsure of themselves, it was a perfect opportunity to say: 'This is horrible. Everything's falling apart. I want out.' This was my gut reaction, despite all the time I'd spent at Daytop, which was over a year and a half. While things were going good, and an essential benevolence was in operation, I could fit in and do my thing. But once things collapsed at the very top, I had a perfect excuse to call it quits and say, 'To hell with it. As I always secretly thought, I'll never make it.' Call it the will toward failure triumphing over the will toward success. Or call it bullshit. Anyway, I went to see one of the assistant directors. He was crying. He was really sad. I wasn't. I was really digging that sense of license and confusion that goes with a crisis. I went back to Swan Lake, but I decided to leave. I went upstairs and packed my bag. I got some money from another guy who was splitting and I called for a cab. Certain people there who thought things would work out asked me to stay. They respected me, they said, and needed my strength. But I said no. Then I got caught in a bit of comic opera that should have brought me to my senses. I was trying to make a resigned and dignified exit. I was halfway down the stairs with my suitcase when it burst open. I dropped it, and my stuff went rolling down the stairs into the front area. By the time I got it all together, I found out that my cab had come and gone. The senior coordinator asked me to stay. I was called into the regional director's office, and he pointed out how long I'd been at Daytop—twenty-one months. Was I going to let all this go down the drain? He said, 'Just wait. We should know soon for sure who's in charge.' I made a compromise. I wanted to go into town, but I promised not to leave the house that night. Instead I brought back a bottle of vodka, even though I didn't feel like drinking. On my return, I found out that it was definite; the old regime was out. The trustees of Daytop had voted to fire David Deitch. We thought it meant that all of us were out too. Almost everybody in the house was drinking. One of my best friends was very drunk and threatened a kid unsympathetic to David Deitch with an empty beer bottle. They were all reverting to their old street roles and raising hell. Everyone sick and selfish and materialistic. The consensus was that we all had a kind of amnesty from the Daytop rules until we got further orders.

"A few nights later I went into town to a night spot called the Lincoln Lounge. Again I was very sneaky about it. Instead of just saying, 'To hell with it. I'm going to get drunk,' I very cagily ordered a couple of drinks, looking around all the time to see who might have spotted me. In case things still worked out, I didn't want anyone to see me drinking in public. I was back in that old ambivalent bag where I didn't want to commit myself one way or the other. Not one of us thought of assuming any responsibility. We didn't want to shoot dope, but we thought we could at least get away with drinking.

"In the next few days we learned that David Deitch was planning to open a new house, but it was all very vague. Those who were on his side would have to leave and fend for themselves as best they could until this project got funded and organized. Daytop itself was being reorganized, but the people I was closest to left, including the ex-resident director and regional director of Swan Lake, who were both married. I decided to go with them, and we all stayed together in a friend's house in Brooklyn. There were three families, with about a dozen kids.

"I'd had a girl friend at Daytop who'd left before the split, and I wanted to see her. She lived out on Long Island. I told the regional director about it, and he said that I shouldn't see her if I wanted to keep my seniority. The pathetic part of this was that, although I'd been at Daytop now for twenty-one months—three months longer than the shortest time one could graduate in—I was still unequipped to deal with the outside world or any situations in it. There was still for me that big gap between Daytop and the outside world. You'd think that because so many people from the outside were involved with Daytop that this exposure would have the same effect as actually being in the outside community. But it didn't. When people came into Daytop to visit, or even to participate in groups, they were on our home turf. The feeling of security was still there. Once outside of Daytop on my own, I was like a scared kid again. The twenty-one months didn't seem to have made any difference.

"I finally ignored the director's advice and sneaked off to see my girl. She had a nice place in Long Island, and I stayed with her. I was in a ridiculous bag at this point. On the one hand, I felt I'd spent so much time at Daytop that if I pulled myself together I could surely make it on my own. On the other hand, I would go out to bars and drink. They were the only places I felt comfortable in, outside of Daytop. My ex-director friends in Brooklyn were disgusted with me. I couldn't make contact with them. They didn't trust me any more. Soon I was drinking every day, and my girl friend was covering for me, trying to get me straightened out. It was so obvious that none of this could be blamed on dope. It was just me, and I was still all screwed up inside, turning scared. I finally got to see the ex-resident director, but he kept pointing an accusing finger at me. I hated feeling guilty again.

"I went back to Boston. Still hung up on booze, I began to take sleeping pills too. I hooked up with another kid named Jimmy who had left Daytop during the split. We went to a friend of his, supposedly to get tranquilizers or barbiturates. The friend wasn't home. We walked around the block. Jimmy said, 'I'd like to cop some stuff.' I said, 'None of that shit for me.' By this time the friend was in. He offered us two bags of heroin. I gave him the money. I didn't want to, but I did anyway. We didn't shoot the stuff. We just snorted it. A real Mickey Mouse operation. I'd done the worst in the least way—it hadn't given me much of a high—just enough to satisfy that old urge to screw myself up. I was so disgusted afterward. I called up my girl. I took a train back to New York and checked in at the Biltmore Hotel. I began sneaking around corners again when I went out, as though somebody was after me. I found a doctor who gave me prescriptions for goof balls and amphetamines. I was trying to get one last good high without actually shooting heroin. But I just started feeling paranoid again. I finally threw away all the pills. I called my girl out on Long Island and told her. 'I'm kicking everything. I need to go back to Daytop.' But I was still scared to confront the new directorship. Instead I went out to stay with her again. She'd stayed clean. She was involved with a new therapeutic concept out there and she had me come in to run some groups. Everybody thought I was terrific, and I even got offered a job to work with them at a high salary. But I felt like a hypocrite. I knew I'd snorted dope. And I'd heard that a warrant was out for me again in Massachusetts for violating my parole.

"So I went to stay with my friends in Brooklyn again. I wasn't sure just what was happening at Daytop, and whether they would take me back. My Brooklyn friends encouraged me to go back, but they didn't want to let me out of the house alone. They knew I was still drinking. I got angry at them for not trusting me. Like a kid again, I made a break for it, and ran down the street. I got my girl from Long Island into the city once more, and we had some drinks together. I knew it was the last time. It was crazy, acting that way, full of certainty about what I needed, but wanting that last bit of freedom. This time I wasn't thinking about sex. I just wanted to see her and say good-bye. I called up Daytop, and they said, 'Okay, whatever shape you're in, we want you back, so get your ass over to Staten Island.'

"Mark Tintrup was the new house director there. I was still so sneaky that I told him all I'd done was a bit of drinking while I was away. Mark told me that he'd take my word for it. They were starting from scratch. They needed strength in the house, and there was a general amnesty on everything except taking heroin. With my seniority, if I'd shot dope, all that would go down the drain again. But I had to tell him. Even though it was snorting, not shooting, it was bad, and he said, 'I'm sorry. That was a stupid thing to do.' But he took me back in the house, saying, 'This is your last chance. I believe in you. Why the hell don't you believe in yourself?'

"Mark was terrific for me. I had to start all over again. But there were no diapers, nothing like that. He knew what my weak smallest things outside of it. David, I think, had wanted Daytop to become some model community, so he discouraged confronting the outside world, which he thought corrupt. Oh, it was point was: being strong at Daytop, but a coward about the rough, going back. Again there was a house meeting, and one of the guys pointed the old finger at me, saying, 'That's a perfect example of what not to be like.' But there was a new emphasis in the house. Mark had me go out to court very soon, helping kids in Daytop who had cases pending or under review. As soon as I was together again, he gave me a lot of outside responsibility. He took a big chance—having me work outside so soon— but it was what I needed. It showed he trusted me and that gave me confidence in myself. He told me not to get too hung up with the dynamics of the house. He knew how good I was at all that, and how little it meant if I was screwed up inside. He had me go out as much as possible on my job. Under the old regime I would have been back at the woodwork in a punishment status. And on my time off, he made me get out in the world, too. I was encouraged to go out on dates with girls, and there was a girl in the house I was really starting to dig. I went to Central Park a few times, to the zoo, things like that. I'd never even seen the Statue of Liberty. How tiny it looked!

"That was almost a year ago. I'm a full coordinator now. I'm not scared of the street any more. I don't feel like a freak. The other night I ran a Saturday-night open house. I was scared stiff, but when it was over they gave me a standing ovation. I'd just been honest with them. I told them what I'd been through and what I was still scared of. I told them how, no matter how high up you get, you still have some of the same feelings as the guy that just got accepted in the house.

"I got no problems when I'm with other people here. I get so much respect and love from these kids that I feel like the strongest guy in the world. It's only when I'm alone sometimes that the old sadness and pain comes over me, and I know my danger is that I can get so involved in my job functions I'll push my own negative feelings back instead of reaching out for the help I still need. I don't mean anything could drive me back to the streets again to shoot dope. But it's hard the higher up you get in Daytop. You're a model for the younger kids, so you can't let them know about your self-doubts, and there's fewer and fewer guys above you or even at your own level. That makes it lonely. And with the kids here—when they love me, is it for me as a person or only because of what I can do for them? Questions like that bother you the higher up you get.

"And won't it be worse if I ever become an assistant director? That's the next step. One of my worst hang-ups has to do with my own son. My wife didn't want him either in the end—too much responsibility—so my parents have been bringing him up. He's six now. Until recently I couldn't even talk to him, his very existence made me feel so anxious. I even tried to convince myself that he wasn't really my kid. But I'm getting over that. The last few months I've been seeing him more often, and we get along. We can talk. He *is* my kid. That girl I mentioned, we've been going together for over a year now, and we'll probably get married once we've both graduated. When that happens, my kid will live with us. I'm still only twenty-seven. There's time. To become a beautiful person. I can see that. But to become a beautiful father. Jesus. The day that happens, I'll know I have it made."

Marilyn

MARILYN'S PARENTS both come from St. Vincent—an island in the British West Indies—but before Marilyn was born they moved to Aruba—a Dutch island just off the coast of Venezuela where the living standard was higher and there were more jobs, due to the presence of a crude oil refinery owned by a subsidiary of Standard Oil of New Jersey. Her father ran the commissary in the white section of the island where the oil people lived and worked. "It was a good job," according to Marilyn. "But it meant that my father was always playing a kind of Uncle Tom role—something I held against him, perhaps unfairly, when I got older. My father's father was white, and my father could almost pass for white, whereas my mother is much darker than I am, a real black. My mother worked too, as a nurse, and we lived in one of the nicest neighborhoods of Oranjestad, the capital, with a good house and a large backyard. The neighbors were all good people, and the atmosphere was very friendly. Relatives and friends were always visiting our house, and at least once a week we had outdoor gatherings—something the equivalent of block parties—where we played records and everybody danced and had things to eat and drink and there was a very warm feeling.

"There were three languages on Aruba, the main one being Dutch, but there were a lot of people like my parents on the island who came from neighboring islands and spoke English. There was also a native dialect called Papiamento, made up of Spanish, Portuguese, and Dutch with smatterings of African, Indian, and even Hebrew, that I could never make head or tail of. My parents were Methodists, but I went to a Catholic school in Aruba because it was the best school there, and, by the time I was ten, I was a top student, getting nineties in every subject. My older sister Ann was five years older than me, and by then she spoke Dutch fluently. My first ambition was to get to speak Dutch as well as she did. It became my favorite subject in school, and in the fifth grade I finished the year as the best student in my class. I can still speak Dutch pretty well now, but my parents never picked up on the language.

"My father worked hard, but he always began drinking when he got home as far back as I can remember. Although he was an alcoholic, he was very punctilious, and he'd never miss a day of work and he'd never go out drinking to bars. But he'd come home and drink every night and there'd often be fights between him and my mother over his drinking and about money and about educating us children. If you think all black West Indians are open, sexually uninhibited people, forget it. Sex was a dirty word in our household, and my mother and father not only slept in separate rooms but at opposite ends of the house. It was always same thing with father. He'd be irritable and crotchety when he got home until he had his first couple of drinks. Then he'd loosen up for a while but, after he'd had too much to drink, he'd get belligerent and irritable again, and it was always impossible to talk to him, drunk or sober. He was really hard on us girls, always suspecting that we were up to no good, especially with boys, and he'd get physically violent. The first beating I remember seeing was on one Saturday morning. Always on Saturday morning, me and my other sister Charlotte, who was two years younger than me, we'd have to do a general cleaning of the house, sometimes about twelve times over—it was even worse than some days at Daytop—and this Saturday morning my father had been up early and drinking and while

40

Charlotte and I were working away in the house, my older sister Ann was out in the yard talking to the son of one of the neighbors through their garage window. When my father found out what she was doing, he told her to get her ass away from that window, and then he got hold of a large anchor rope and proceeded to beat the hell out of her—all for talking to a neighbor's son through a garage window. That was the first bad beating I ever saw, and it scared the hell out of me, and it also made me despise my father a little. Of course, whatever kind of a mood my father was in from drinking, as soon as the doorbell rang, he'd put on a real friendly social appearance and be just as nice as he could be. That's the way he seemed to most of our friends and neighbors, real friendly and respectable. And that's the way he must have seemed at work, or he never would have been able to hold down that good job: a real friendly, dignified gentleman.

"There were so many fights between him and my mother that it sometimes seems there was nothing else, and it's hard to remember any quiet evenings at home where we all just sat around and relaxed and had a good time. Usually there had to be visitors in the house before there could be a relaxed atmosphere. One of the weirdest fights was the time my mother became convinced she was dying. We were all in the dining room together after supper, and they were arguing, as usual, about money. My father would work out the budget, but it was my mother who had the actual money and who cashed his paycheck. It was something about this financial system they were arguing about. My mother didn't usually fight back against him physically, but this night she picked up a dish off the dinner table and hurled it at him, she was so angry. In return, he tried to hit her, and then my mother sort of passed out or fainted, and the doctor came over and said that she had very high blood pressure and she was bundled off into her room, and the whole atmosphere became very serious with a friend staying with her through the night and my father brooding apart and drinking. And in the morning my mother called me into her, and she talked very faintly as though she were about to expire any moment, and she mumbled to me about something in her desk that she wanted me to have, as though it were a death-bed present, and then there was the doctor and my father in the room forcing some food down her throat because she refused to eat, and then shortly the whole crisis was over, and to this day my mother's never told me what it was she wanted to give me—back there on her death bed!

"Aside from the fighting at home, I loved Aruba. I want to go back after I graduate from Daytop and spend some time there, once I'm straightened out. Of course I can't tell if I'd want to live there. I just might not fit in after everything that's happened with me in this country. I've had American citizenship papers around a long time—but something's always stopped me from going ahead and filling them out. I've got bad feelings about this country. A lot of it's the trouble I got into with drugs. But more of it has to do with my being black and all the prejudice here. Although good things have happened to me here too, like Daytop, I like knowing that behind everything my own country is Aruba. This is something I'll have to work out real slowly, but I'm in no hurry.

"We'd have some great times on that island, especially on weekends. My father had this old green 1948 Plymouth that he was real proud of and taught my mother to drive. We'd go over every day during the week and pick him up after work. Then on weekends, if my father wasn't in too bad a mood, we'd pick up and go driving out to the beach or up into the country. The beach had these beautiful palm trees and every family we knew had its own favorite tree where they'd spread out their blankets and picnic things and lie and loaf in the shade. When it was too hot on the beaches, we used to drive into the country and pick wild grapes bigger than cherries. We had grapes in our own backyard, but they were never as delicious as the wild grapes. I liked all that tropical fruit—the mangoes and especially the jellied coconuts that grew on some of the palm trees. They weren't like the coconuts we get here where inside there's milk but the fruit is very hard. The fruit of the jellied coconuts is delicious and soft—almost like custard, and very sweet. I always loved to eat, especially sweet things. My first addiction was to sweets. That's a fact. I clearly remember that when I was eleven years old I weighed ninety pounds! The only time I was ever thin was when I was on heroin. But to get back to Aruba. You had this real community feeling there. Everyone talks about community here, but there really isn't any. The whole island was like one huge family. At Christmastime, for instance, almost everybody exchanged presents with everybody. Nothing expensive, but it was out of sight, all those little gifts. Yeah. Christmas. It reminds me of Black Pete.

"In Aruba we don't have Santa Claus. Instead, like in the Netherlands, we have St. Nicholas. But St. Nicholas is white, so we also have Black Pete. Black Pete is St. Nicholas' sidekick, helps him out on his rounds. Jesus, I'm considered something of a black militant around here, and here I am getting nostalgic about Black Pete! What I wanted to tell you about was the family feeling on the island. Now dig this. I used to sometimes borrow things belonging to my mother, without her knowledge. You could call it temporary stealing. See? If you look at me from a psychological point of view, here I am by the age of ten already stealing from my mother and already addicted to sweets. The seeds of my criminal career, the pattern, were already planted. Got it? So one day I took this gold bracelet of my mother's. It was inlaid with small diamonds and quite valuable. I took it into town and lost it. I was terrified of what my mother would do to me, but by the time I got home the bracelet had already been returned. Somebody'd found it on the street and recognized it as my mother's! That's how Aruba was."

Although things were so good in Aruba, Marilyn's mother was anxious for the three girls to get a higher education. "The schools in Aruba," Marilyn explained, "only went up through the tenth grade. And my older sister Ann was now about to graduate. The first arrangement was that Ann would go to Grenada—that's an English island—where she could study languages, but it turned out to be too expensive. My parents were also checking out the possibilities of going to Holland or of sending Ann there. There'd be endless discussions and arguments over every angle of every plan. Basically, my father had a very good job in Aruba. He knew it would be hard to get as good a job anywhere else, and he was against all of us moving. It was really my mother who wanted to leave. She kept accusing my father of being selfish about not wanting to go. She said he was putting his own comfort above the needs of us children. She was full of this idea that nothing mattered except that we get a good education. Sometime before, as a possibility, they'd applied for visas to the United States, and just at this time, when they were trying to decide what to do, these visas came through, and that settled it. We'd go to New York. An aunt of mine had already gone to Brooklyn, and we would stay with her until we could find a house of our own and get settled. All this was going to happen in about two weeks! I was twelve then. It was 1958. I was terribly excited. I'd never been out of Aruba, and I thought of America as this great adventurous place where there'd be lots of open spaces and horses and cowboys. I couldn't wait to get here. It was during Easter holidays, and the rush was on so that we'd be able to start school in New York at the beginning of a new term—after Easter vacation. I didn't feel sad to leave Aruba at all. I remember, though, that I felt bad because I'd borrowed a pen from a girl at school before Easter holidays—and now I'd never be back in school to return it to her.

"When the big day came, I was only sad because we were leaving our dog Rex behind. But I wasn't anywhere near as sad as the dog. My father was coming with us for several weeks to help us get set up. Then he was going back to Aruba for another year or so. If he could stick it out that long alone, he'd get some pension benefits from his job in the oil community.

"We had a ball on the plane coming up. Me and Charlotte played games and ran back and forth and the stewardesses loved us, and we all had a feeling that an exciting new life was about to start. Aruba was nice, but it wasn't the most exciting place in the world. I was carrying this little blue jacket I'd been given for Easter. I guess my mother had no idea how cold New York would be that time of year. The trip took seven or eight hours. When we landed, it was snowing hard. We'd never even *felt* cold before, much less seen any snow. We were fascinated and slid around on patches of ice while we were waiting to get through customs. There was some delay because my father was

44

bringing in a whole lot of liquor. It's very cheap in Aruba, much less than in New York, so he had that angle all figured out. When we finally got through, my aunt was waiting for us, and we took the limousine into Manhattan. We were really bowled over by all the big buildings and everything, but I remember feeling a little closed in on that trip from the airport because I'd never ridden in a car before with the windows closed. In Manhattan we transferred to the Seventh Avenue subway. I'd never been on a train before, and it went so fast I was scared it wouldn't stay on the tracks. When we got to my aunt's home in Brownsville, there was a big welcoming party, and all the kids were allowed to stay up late. The television was going. I'd seen TV before but only in a store."

When Easter vacation was over, and Marilyn's parents started looking for a house to buy, she began going to P.S. 282, which was only four blocks from her aunt's house. She felt very lonely. Outside the school she and Charlotte had to stand in different lines to sign up for classes, and neither one of them had ever stood in a line before. Marilyn's lips were chapped and she had a handkerchief over her mouth to keep out the cold. "I was standing exactly in line," said Marilyn, "and all of a sudden this bigshot student guard wearing a special white belt comes over to me and says, 'What the hell do you think you're doing?' and he rips the handkerchief away from my mouth. I didn't take any crap from anybody, even when I was twelve, so I proceeded to tell him off, and we probably would have gotten into a fist fight if a teacher hadn't come over and broken it up."

Marilyn started in on the final term of the fifth grade. Because of what she'd learned in Aruba, she was way ahead of the other kids in her class. "That school was unbelievable," she said. "I never had the heart to tell my parents what it was like, they were so full of propaganda about American education. I had this weirdo teacher with red hair and buck teeth and glasses, and he kept saying in this conciliatory manner, 'Now, fellas, now, girls,' but he took absolutely everything that went on in that class. It was crazy. Kids would be feeling each other up and necking while lessons were going on, and it wasn't unusual for them to be screwing on the floor behind the last row of desks.

There were older guys in the class who'd been repeating the work for about three years in a row, and they had all the younger guys and girls looking up to them. It was sheer lunacy. I was ahead of them all in everything except American history, but I caught up on that pretty fast—the whole year's work—and ended up getting nineties in every subject on my first report card."

But Marilyn's hard work did not help her to feel accepted. Her classmates regarded her as something of a square for not joining into the sexual antics, for getting good grades, and they poked fun at her West Indian accent. People had always liked her before, and she couldn't get used to her new role as an outsider. "For one thing," she said, "I vowed to get rid of every trace of my West Indian accent. It was like learning to talk all over again, and I'd practice for hours at home, getting the lilt out of my voice. It didn't take me long, and in the end it was like English for me was two languages—the one I used at school and the one I used at home. It's still that way, and I talk the old Caribbean English when I'm with my family."

After a couple of months her family moved into their own house. It was in a middle class neighborhood—the Lincoln Place section of Park Slope near Prospect Park. They'd bought the house. It had four stories and a basement floor. They planned to rent the top two floors. "It's changed now," said Marilyn. "But at that time we were the only black people on our block. It was a quiet neighborhood with no commotion, no gang fights on the street, like in Brownsville. The house needed a lot of work, but it was worth it. We all pitched in, fixing the place up, and things seemed promising again. I transferred to P.S. 4 before the end of the term, a considerable improvement in every way over the school in Brownsville. When school let out, I helped at home, but I also got to know many of the kids in the neighborhood. My father had gone back to Aruba to work, and my mother was more lenient with me, so some of the pressure was off. I had a good time. My father wrote to all of us—Ann, Charlotte, my mother, and me—but I think I was the only one who wrote back.

"While still in Brownsville I used to steal change from my

father when he refused to give me any. I took money from my mother too. She'd started working in a hospital, and she had a new hair style. She had long straight hair she was very proud of, and I'd comb it out for her every morning before she went to work. One day I snatched a bill out of her wallet while it was lying on the bed. I thought it was just a single, but it turned out to be a five. I bought candy and soft drinks with it and, yeah, I tried to feel good about the whole thing, pretended I didn't feel guilty at all, that I had it coming to me. When my mother found it missing, and asked me if I'd taken it, I said, 'No. Definitely not.' I never had any allowance, and the most money my mother ever gave me was a dime. Since I wouldn't cop to taking the money, all three of us got beaten for it. Now my sisters each knew they hadn't taken it, so the culprit had to be me, and they wouldn't let the issue fizzle out. They kept the pressure up so long that I finally ended up copping to it. My mother was so angry and upset! If it sounds trivial, remember that my mother was very straitlaced and religious and hard-working, and I was probably closest to her of all us kids. She took me downstairs and spanked the hell out of me—it was with a cheese-grater no less— and told me to pray to God to forgive me. I got twelve cheese-grater lashings. Then she wrote to my father and told him all about it. It was strange. Instead of scolding me, he wrote and told me very calmly that I didn't have to steal if there were things I needed. And he enclosed ten dollars! I think he was soft on me because he was lonely down there in Aruba. I stopped stealing from my mother but only briefly. I soon found a roll of bills my mother had hidden which came from tips patients gave her. She had the amounts written down, but I'd just change the figures and take what I needed. Once I took twenty dollars within two days. I bought toys for my friends, which made me feel important and good. I wanted a hula hoop but I was scared to buy one in case my mother might wonder where I'd gotten the money. I was her favorite daughter. I talked to her a lot, and if she was sick it was me who made breakfast and did the household chores."

In the seventeen years that her parents had been married, this was the first time, according to Marilyn, that her father had been away from home. Back in Aruba, he'd sold their old house and was living in a rented room in the home of some neighbors. He was supposed to stay put until the following summer—of 1959—so he'd get that pension. But at five o'clock one afternoon, Marilyn was out in the yard playing with a hula hoop—she'd finally managed to get one legitimately—when the doorbell rang. Marilyn answered it and found her father standing there with all his bags. "I was genuinely happy to see him," said Marilyn. "I gave him a real warm and loving welcome, but he was uptight and I could tell that something was wrong, that he'd showed up just a little too soon. All I know is that immediately he and my mother went upstairs to talk, leaving us to do our homework, and we heard this terrible quarrel going on. My mother was furious and they were screaming at each other, and in this instance I couldn't help being on my father's side. He'd been lonely, and he wanted to be with us, and he'd come home, and here was my mother not even acting glad to see him, but only screaming about money. I didn't understand what the issue was all about. Ann was a better spy, and through her I finally fitted all the pieces together. The basic issue was this: the pension, however small, would have been a guaranteed income for life. So he blew it all by leaving too soon. It was stupid, but I couldn't help feeling for him, whereas my mother didn't get over being angry at him for months. It wasn't as though we were that poor.

"Meanwhile I was still doing well at school. It was a much better place—P.S. 4—than the school in Brownsville, and both Charlotte and I got very high marks. I was about the best student in the sixth grade, and even my father was very proud of me. But his big hang-up was that he was prejudiced against black Americans, and this was always causing friction. When we'd first moved to our new house, we were the only black people on the block, but now there were a few other black families, and I'd made friends with this black girl, Angela, who lived across the street. One day she was visiting me, and my father comes home and says right in front of her, 'Get this black bitch out of here!' When she's gone, he then proceeds to tell me how if I hang out with the black girls in the neighborhood, I'll eventually sink down to their level and end up being a prostitute. The crazy thing about it was that Angela had lighter skin than my own mother. I really hated him for that."

Marilyn added, though, that this needling from her father, however obnoxious, had little to do with her later turning to prostitution. "I never wanted to hustle, and I avoided it for as long as I could, as long as I was getting dope from my boyfriends. Don't forget my background was practically middle class in terms of values. We were well off, despite all my mother's complainings. We owned our own home. I wasn't a ghetto kid. I guess after I'd been hustling awhile, there'd be some satisfaction in saying to my father, 'You always told me I'd be a prostitute, and now that's what I am.' But that doesn't mean his attitude was the cause of my hustling. At Daytop we don't believe much in so-called psychological motivations. Let people interpret it any way they want. All I know is I ended up hustling because I needed the money to buy dope, and my boyfriend had gone to jail. That seemed the easiest way. It's more convenient than stealing, and the penalties, even if you get caught, are much less. Ninety days and you're out again. Anyway, I was never arrested for prostitution.

"But to get back to my father: great conferences were held about what he should do, now that he was in New York without a job. Of course he'd known all along that he'd never get a job like the one he had down in Aruba. This he could hold against my mother, since coming to New York was her idea. And she still held against him the fact that he'd goofed and lost that pension. So it went. Actually, it was pretty sad. He ended up taking a job as a packer in a supermarket, and he wasn't used to that kind of work. He'd come from this real warm climate, and they put him to work in cold storage where he had to handle frozen goods. From the cold his hands got all messed up with sores and blisters that got badly infected, but he was too proud to complain, and he ended up having to quit and being out of work for three or four months. My father was also a diabetic, and don't ask me how he got along all that time drinking the way he did every night. It's a mystery. I guess he had a good constitution beneath it all. After he got his hands cleared up, he

49

went to work as a file clerk with a cardboard and paper company. It was better than the supermarket job, but he had this horrible slob for a boss who weighed about 300 pounds and smelled like a tub of grease. My father gave this open house one night and invited his boss to it, along with other white people that worked with him. He didn't want black people in the house, but he'd invite that fat slob over and make a big production of it. Talk about kissing Whitey's ass! I could have killed my father for that—it was really disgusting."

It was in the seventh grade that Marilyn's marks started going down. She wouldn't do much homework. She felt defiant and stubborn. Her father kept yelling at her about bringing black whores into the house, when all the time it was just her girl friend Angela. Marilyn, in retaliation, would say, 'To hell with him. I'll just sit around and watch TV.' Her mother would encourage her to study, but Marilyn paid no attention, and she was stealing from her parents whatever she could. When she got caught again, her father delivered a long lecture on the evils of stealing, but it only inspired her to devise more subtle and foolproof methods. At this time she only took a few dollars a week, just enough to keep her in candy and spending money. In any case, it was hard for her to get out of the house long enough to spend very much. Her parents were reluctant to let her out of sight, especially at night. "I guess they figured that would keep me out of trouble," said Marilyn, "but it was only building up pressure inside me to rebel completely.

"By the time I got to eighth grade, I didn't feel close to anybody in school either. I'd gotten rid of my West Indian accent, but that wasn't enough. I didn't feel part of the scene, and I wasn't too happy about myself. I didn't like my being fat and having freckles, and I was jealous of my younger sister Charlotte because she was prettier than me. And from all the sweets I ate, my teeth were starting to go bad. I think I had at least one cavity in every tooth! One night I had a bad toothache. We rented out the top floor apartment of our house, and the girl who lived up there introduced me to my first wine. She said it would ease the pain. Then I went downstairs and drank some of my father's whiskey. It tasted terrible, but I liked the feeling. I had a couple more shots, holding my nose, to get the stuff down, and then I went outside and sat on the steps of our house. I felt real free and unself-conscious and started talking a blue streak with people passing by. I felt casual and close to everybody, like I belonged. Then I got very sleepy. It was a little weird, but it was nice.

"I began taking wine to school and drinking it in the bathroom and sharing it with a few of the older girls. It was pretty stupid, but it had been a long time since I'd been at the center of things, and there I was every day, real cool and defiant, the head of the drinkers in the eighth grade toilet. I thought I was really swinging! Things were looking up! I had some kind of *thing* going, and I was coming into my own. Then one day my social status got a big boost. It could have been my undoing, but it worked out great. My sister Charlotte got into a fight with the younger sister of the toughest girl in our class, a kind of female gang leader named Marty. They had this code that older sisters had to defend the honor of their kid sisters, and before I knew it, this girl Marty was out for me, and there was no way I could get out of it. I met her on the school stairs, and she suddenly lashed out at me. I got the message and dragged her down the stairs as she hit me. We began brawling, but a teacher came along and broke it up. The principal called me down and gave me a lecture, but Marty had a reputation there as a big troublemaker, so they figured it was more her fault. By this time, Charlotte and Marty's kid sister had patched things up, but the whole thing had escalated, and I got the word that Marty would be waiting for me outside the school at three o'clock with her gang to give me a going-over. Jesus, was I scared, but I didn't show it. I took a few shots of wine and began to talk big, about how I had this machete in my locker and was going to cut her up good if she tried anything. It was such a good act I began to fall for it myself. Then just before school lets out, this meeting is arranged between Marty and myself, and she explains that she's in real serious trouble in the school, so she's going to have to call the whole thing off, at least for that day. I pretend that I don't give a damn one way or the other, and we end up being good friends.

"The next summer I drank a lot. My grades had been going

51

down, and in the eighth grade I flunked the new math. I was cutting a lot of classes and getting into all sorts of disciplinary trouble. My teeth were giving me trouble, and my father had put up about $500 in advance to a dentist to have them all fixed. When he found out that I hadn't even gone to the dentist once, he blew his stack.

"I started high school at Prospect Heights, which was an all-girl school. This was in the fall of 1961. I was fifteen. Angela went there already, and Charlotte planned to come the following year. She was always one year behind me.

"In the tenth grade, when Charlotte came, I used to bring bottles of wine and whiskey to school in my school bag—Gypsie Rose Wine and Johnny Walker Red Label. We used to raise as much hell as we possibly could. I'd often call up and say there was a bomb planted in the school. That would keep the kids out of school for at least an hour. I was drunk much of the time. On the day before Christmas vacation we decided to burn the whole damn school down. There were ten of us. Some brought gasoline, the others, rolls and rolls of newspaper. We spread the papers and poured out all the gasoline, and were about to light it up when a teacher smelled the gasoline and sounded the alarm. We got away, ran into our classes, and they never did catch us. In the eleventh grade, I only went to school nineteen times, and was expelled at the end of the school year for absenteeism.

"When I was expelled, my father helped me get into John Jay High School. The dean said no, but I was a good actress and made a favorable impression on the principal, who decided to give me a chance. I showed up for two days, but the third day I got drunk and stayed home. Charlotte wanted to transfer to John Jay too, but my father said no. We were a bad influence on each other. But Charlotte threatened to leave school and home too, so my father, in the end, had to give his permission.

"This meant that Charlotte and I and a couple of other friends were together again. We began to raise hell, and I'd only show up a few days each week. I had another peculiarity. I hated to get to school early. It made me feel embarrassed, like I was on display. So I always tried to get to school late, which had other advantages. No crowded buses. This was the year I started going to St. John's Place and hanging around with older guys around twenty-eight and twenty-nine.

"At first I was very puritanical about pot—like most lushes— and I never even imagined taking heroin. Then one day this kid Benny from St. John's Place brought a bag of pot over to my house. I thought you could get a habit from smoking pot, but Benny straightened me out on that score, and I decided to try it. Now you hear a lot of stories about people getting sick or feeling nothing the first time they smoke pot. But that wasn't the case with me. Benny showed me how to hold the smoke in my lungs. I got stoned the first time, and I felt good. From then on it was normal for me to take at least a few reefers and a bottle of wine a day.

"I was still going to school off and on. But they didn't want to put me in the twelfth grade the next year because of my low grades. They wanted me to repeat the eleventh grade *again*. That would be the third time around. This was bad enough. Then, on the last day of school, I was in the bathroom swigging some wine and smoking a reefer when I got caught by a teacher's aide. She reported me to the principal, and I was told that I would be expelled. I would have to go home and tell my parents and bring them back with me to sign some papers. Now I'd recently gotten in the habit of stealing checks from my parents and cashing them at Bohack's where I was known. I'd just cashed a check for $25 that morning, so I was loaded. I didn't know what the hell to do. I was confused and depressed about myself. I knew I'd brought all this on myself, but that just made it worse. I thought of running away from home, but I didn't quite have the guts to do that. I couldn't face the changes that would involve.

"I bought two bottles of wine and then I went to a druggist that knew me and bought a bottle of sleeping pills under the counter. I went to a park bench, took a couple of pills, and drank some wine with a guy I knew. Then I went to see another friend at St. John's Place, where I took some more sleeping pills and eventually passed out in the bathroom. What happened after that I don't remember, but I got a general picture the following morning from various friends and my sisters. My boyfriend, Ronnie, and another friend got me home. My parents wanted to get me to a hospital, but, on the other hand, they were afraid that I'd get put away, so they decided to try to keep me awake instead, which was not difficult. I picked up a scarf from the dresser and began to thump and leap around the room, making out like a Spanish flamenco dancer. I kidded my father about his drinking and his prejudices against black people in a kind of running comic monologue which was quite impressive. Then I told everybody 'I won't do it again. It was just one of those things,' half-talking and half-singing, so that my parents figured I must be okay and it wouldn't be necessary to get me to a hospital. Then I told everybody I loved them and that everything was going to be okay someday, and I went to sleep. By this time, word of my escapade had gotten around to my friends in various versions, one of them being that I was dead and that the wake had already started. So when my friends arrived, wanting to know what the score was, Ann covered me up with a blanket, put on a sobbing act, and told them all, 'Yes. She's dead. It's all over. Please leave us alone until tomorrow.'

"The next morning I had no hangover at all. I felt terrific and went to school. I felt great because the kids who thought I was dead were happy to see me. I guess that's all I was trying to prove with that crazy stunt. I wanted to see if my friends liked me enough to want me alive. My parents found out about my stealing checks, but they were too scared of what I might do next to say anything. They just told Bohack's not to cash any more checks for me. That's all. When you start acting really crazy, you can have your parents over a barrel."

Marilyn felt temporarily purged of her hostility and restlessness, following the sleeping pill incident, and resolved to play it straight for a while. She got a job as a nurse's aide in a Jewish old-age home. "They weren't too badly off," said Marilyn. "They were just lonely like I was and emotionally messed up. We got along good, though, and I'd do extra little things to make them feel happy. But although I treated them well, I didn't take the job seriously. I treated it all like a joke. That was my big bag, even after I came to Daytop—being real cool and laughing everything off. Playing the clown all the time,

I didn't have to feel all the pain inside me. So my attempt to settle down in this job didn't mean much. I was always late getting to work, and soon I was getting stoned again almost every night. I quit the job, and I'd get out of the house as early as I could every morning, pretending that I was looking for a job. I never kept any appointments. I never *made* any appointments. The most I might do, which I thought was quite a concession, was to make a very tentative phone call about some job, pretending I was very interested and would be right over.

"In the meantime, pressures at home were building up toward a new explosion which killed off every trace of communication between my father and me. I'd just turned eighteen. Some friends were going to give me a small party. But I didn't know it then. It was supposed to be a surprise. This guy I was going with, he just said he wanted to take me out, so I didn't know there was a party planned. On top of that, the last time I'd talked to him over the phone, my father had grabbed the receiver away from me and told this guy, 'Get the hell off my phone, motherfucker!' Because of that, I wasn't too anxious to keep the date with this guy, and I figured he might not show up anyway. Instead, I went to the liquor store, bought a bottle, and went to visit another boyfriend of mine. My sister Charlotte was with me, and we sat around rapping and drinking and smoking pot, and suddenly it was very late, and Charlotte and I left. Charlotte said she was going home, but I was beginning to feel bad about the guy I hadn't kept the date with, and decided I'd go over and straighten things out with him. I ended up staying the night there and didn't wake up until ten o'clock the next morning. What I didn't know was that my father, all riled up because we were out so late, beat the hell out of Charlotte while she was still in bed, and he was now just waiting to get his hands on me. I was planning to sneak into the house long enough to get my bathing suit, and then I was going to Coney Island with my boyfriend. I knocked on the door, Ann let me in, and I asked her to lend me a dollar. I was in the bathroom upstairs where the tenants lived, when my father began beating on the door. Ann had squealed on me—something she'd never done before. My father was insane with rage. What

I did was to pull the bathroom door open real quick, so that my father would fall in and I could get around him while he was still off balance. The trick worked, and I got behind him, but I wasn't quite quick enough. My father caught up with me on the stairs, and Ann helped him hold me down, while he began to beat me with his fists. Then my mother got into the act, trying to tie my feet up with rope. My father was cursing me and punching me, and I began screaming bloody murder, and my screams were so loud, and my father was hitting me so hard that Charlotte downstairs got frightened and called the police. I was cursing my father back, and I was so angry now that I wouldn't give up, no matter what he did to me, and he didn't stop until the doorbell rang. The police took my father's side, because they knew him, and they knew me from the days when I used to play hooky from school week after week. Things quieted down, but I was filled with a kind of numb rage against my father. I told him, 'I'm getting the hell out of this house. I'm never calling you Daddy again. And if you ever touch me again, so help me God, I'll kill you.' I meant it. Both my eyes were all swollen up, my lips were bleeding, and there were belts and lumps all over my face. Out on the street, I ran into a guy, a real quiet type I didn't know very well. We sat in the school park awhile, and he said I could live in a room at his place, or if I didn't like that idea, he was sure I could stay a while with his sister. I said thanks, I'd think it over, and then I went and told my boyfriend Ronnie what had happened, and he suggested I come and live with him. I went to visit a few other friends, and they all offered me a place to stay, but I don't know. I couldn't quite see it. I was scared to pull out of the home scene completely, so I ended up going back. Maybe I knew, too, that my father had acted so bad that I had him over a barrel now. And I could always get around my mother. I kept my word. I wouldn't talk to my father at all. He threatened once to hit me again, and I broke a beer bottle and wielded it at him, and told him that if he so much as touched me, I'd cut him to pieces. They didn't know what to do with me after that. I came and went as I pleased. Sometimes I'd stay away for two or three days at a time, and they'd leave me

56

alone. That's what I wanted. But I hated them. And I hated myself and my friends, and I didn't have any hope about anything."

Meanwhile the family upstairs had moved out, and a black tenant named Warren had moved in. Marilyn was nineteen now, and Warren was thirty-seven. "I thought of him as a dirty old man," said Marilyn. "But I'd heard he shot dope, and that intrigued me. One day I went up to see him, and he asked me to go out with him to cash a check. We went to a hotel near Fort Greene in Brooklyn. I thought he was trying to make out with me, but all he was interested in was getting the change back from this check. We went up in the room for a while and drank some wine. He told me, 'I dig you, baby, let's make it.' I couldn't quite see it, but I went along with the idea. There was something about him I liked. But he was on dope and couldn't get it up. That gave me a chance to put him down as a man and revert to my old clowning, tough-girl bag, and I said to him, like I was real experienced, 'I don't know when the hell you'll be ready to come, but I got to go!' I had $20 on me, and he said to me, 'Lend me the twenty tonight, and I'll pay you back thirty tomorrow.' I gave it to him and stayed around awhile. Then a friend of his named Ford came over, and he told me, 'Warren has nice stuff. Try it sometime.'

"A few days later I went up to Warren's apartment and asked him for a fix. I wanted to try it. He told me how bad a heroin habit was, but I didn't put much stock in that because I knew he was hooked himself. He didn't want to do it. But I finally told him that I'd tell my parents he was a dope fiend if he didn't fix me up. He did, and I liked it, but he must have given me a very weak shot. I came down the stairs itching. My kid sister had already tried heroin on her own, and the next time, we both went upstairs to score off Warren. He owed my parents several weeks' rent, and, just about then, he decided to take the cure at Manhattan General Hospital. My parents liked him, and they trusted him to pay the rent whenever he could. They still didn't know that he was an addict or that he was going to take the cure. The next thing I knew, he was out of the hospital and phoning me from a small upstate hotel in a town called

Mountaindale where he had a job as a waiter. They were just opening up for the season and needed more help, so he suggested I work up there during the summer as a maid. Charlotte was fed up with New York, too, and she said she'd like to go up there with me. My parents were against it, but Warren convinced them that it would be good for us both to get out of the city, that it was a healthy environment, and that we could make good money. Of course my parents had no idea there was anything going on between Warren and me. They thought of him as a very responsible, fatherly person. They finally consented. I went up the end of June.

"The first night I got there, Warren and I went to bed together. He had two bottles of booze and some reefers. All we had to do that week was get the hotel open. We went to bed together the next night too. It was a beautiful setup. Charlotte liked it too. The three of us ran the place. When it got busy, the owners would bring in extra help. We all got along nice together. Both Warren and me were saving money, so we bought a car and began driving down to New York after work. The idea was that we were going down to pick up a little pot, but our real motive was to score for some stuff. Warren had been married to this junkie broad. They'd been separated for thirteen years, but he was still very close and friendly with his mother-in-law and brother-in-law who lived up around 128th Street. We scored off them and went up to the roof, but Warren had taken too strong a dose, seeing as how he'd been off stuff for several weeks. He was bombed out of his mind, but he insisted on driving. He crashed into the rear end of another car, while he was nodding at the wheel. We had an open bottle of whiskey in the car, and I managed to get it out just before a cop came over, and Warren got himself together. We went back to his mother-in-law's, but they didn't have room for us to stay the night, so we drove all the way back to the hotel, both of us drunk and high, and from then on we'd make the same trip at least once every week.

"We came down the next week, only we ran out of money in New York, and, on the way back to the hotel, we ran out of gas, two towns away from Mountaindale. That was really horrible! It was around three in the morning, and we were stuck on some backwoods road we'd been taking as a shortcut to save gas. We were so thirsty we were gagging, and we didn't even have any water. The next morning the hotel people drove over and got us. They were happy to see us, and that was nice. We got real close to that family and we stayed on there until the middle of October. We even went to the bar mitzvah of their son, like one of the family. We didn't want to leave when the time came. I'd also lost weight up there, and that made me feel good.

"When we got back to New York, we were rolling in money. We got a three-room apartment in Brooklyn not too far from my family. Of course they were furious. Warren began going out a lot. He said he was driving a taxicab part-time, and he'd bring all these guys home with him late at night. What chaos! Everybody was high on pot or stuff. I told him to cut it out, but he didn't, and I stuck with him anyway. We needed furniture, so I went to a store and bought it and charged it under a phony name. Warren had a brother who'd been cashing bad checks, and the cops were looking for him. The brother had dropped out of sight, but Warren looked like him, so the cops busted Warren and found some stuff on him, and it was suddenly up to me to bail him out. If we'd had the money, I wouldn't have charged the furniture under a phony name, so I was broke, with Warren in jail, and the same day all this furniture arrives. What to do? I asked my mother to lend me the $200 bail on the strength of the furniture, which I said I'd turn over to her if I couldn't make the debt good within thirty days. They didn't know that the furniture, in effect, was stolen, so they said okay. It was worth a lot more than $200, so they must have figured they were getting a pretty good deal.

"In the meantime, a friend of Warren's, named Roy, told me that he'd take care of me until Warren got back on the scene. He was dealing pot—a good brand called Panama Red. What he did was to deal pot so that he'd have enough money to buy heroin. The idea was to sell all the pot he had on him, before driving uptown in my car to score for stuff. He asked me to come with him. I tried to discourage him, because he'd just had his driving license revoked. But he said to hell with that, he couldn't be unlucky two days in a row. All right, I said, so we started driving up Flatbush Avenue, and the next thing I know we're in a collision, and the cops are everywhere, wanting to know everything. Although the car was under my name, I'd given my mother the registration as partial security for the $200, so we had to call her up. That was cleared, but Roy got a summons for driving without a license. It was just at this point that Warren suddenly showed up, strolling down Flatbush Avenue, as if everything was okay.

"We had no money and no home, so Warren stayed awhile with his friends and I moved back in with my family. I was feeling pretty sick at this time. I was getting strung out, and I wasn't eating. I was throwing up all the time—mostly liquids—and I was very dehydrated. When Warren got a small apartment on Sixth Avenue, I moved back in with him. Now I was shooting dope every day, and so was Warren. We were dealing too—just enough to support our own habits. A bunch of Warren's friends often came to our place to cop, and we had six sets of works in the place. But the police were starting to nose around, so we had to move out. Again I went home. That gave me a chance to get at the keys to the new locks my mother had had installed. Once I had copies of the keys made, I began breaking into my parents' house during the day to steal whatever I could get my hands on—rugs, vacuum cleaners, and cash—cash was often around because my parents were suspicious of banks. For a while we had quite a game going there—my parents installing all sorts of new and complex locks on all the doors and windows. The place was like a small fortress—armed against me. The strange thing was that when I went home on social visits I'd deny that I had anything to do with the stuff that was missing—and my father was in such a rage by now that my mother was inclined to go easy on me, even though she knew what the score was. I guess she didn't want to lose contact with me completely. She was probably afraid I might kill myself with an overdose."

One day Marilyn broke in and found the key to her mother's personal strongbox—a prize which had previously eluded her. In it was $500, of which she took $200. "When my mother found it missing, she accused me, but of course I denied everything," said Marilyn. "My mother figured it was time to stop being suspicious of banks, and she gave the other $300 to my father to take to the bank. Now dig this. Later that night he passed out, and when he came to, the money was missing. Naturally, he blamed it on me. Since I happened to be innocent this time, the accusation made me angry and I began looking for the money all over the house. At last I found it. Where? Under my father's bed—it must have fallen out of his pocket. But what the hell? He already thought I'd taken it, so now I did. That got Warren and me together again in a nice hotel room, and when that ran out I had this emerald ring that some guy had given my sister Charlotte. It had a crack in it, and I'd always figured it was worthless. I took it to a pawnshop along with a watch—for which I got $10. By this time Warren had come back with a bundle—that's thirty bags of stuff. We took off, and just then the telephone rang. It was the pawnbroker offering us $600 if we'd sell the ring outright. Jesus. We thought that would be enough to retire on. It lasted about two weeks. We were broke again, and nothing was going right. We were really strung out now. Together we were shooting about thirty bags a day—five times a day—three bags in every shot. This girl I knew was always trying to get me to hustle. I'd always said no before, but this night I thought I'd give it a try. She took me out to Fourth Avenue around midnight, and she had me watch while she picked a guy up. She explained that after a while you could build up a string of regular tricks and that it wasn't so bad. I watched her approach this guy and say, 'Hi, sweetie, you want to have some fun tonight?' She waved at me, smiling, as she went off with the guy. When she came back, she said, 'See? It's simple. Now you try it.' I was shaking all over, but I approached this guy and used exactly the same phrasing she had. Only I asked for $20 and $2, instead of $10 and $2. That was $20 for the trick and $2 for the room. He knew I was new at the game, but he was nice about it. By the time we got to the room I was scared half to death. But it wasn't so bad, and I was sort of pleased with myself for having the guts to go through with it.

He kidded me and told me I was just a little girl angry at my mother. I ended up making almost $200 my first night on the street. Warren objected at first, but eventually he went along with it."

Marilyn started going out on the street every night. She and Warren were living together in a hotel. He was still out on bail from the time he'd gotten busted. He was dealing a lot, and the cops were looking for him. They both knew it was just a matter of time before they caught up with him. One day he went out to sell his last bag before going uptown to score himself, and he never came back. Marilyn went to see him once in court. This time they were holding him on $10,000 bail on a charge of selling, and there was no way of raising that much. He was convicted of selling heroin and got a five-year sentence.

Marilyn's younger sister, Charlotte, was hustling on her own by this time and soon they decided to work the streets together. "She was seventeen and I was nineteen," said Marilyn. "We were the youngest prostitutes on the block, and we were very popular. We made a lot of money, and I didn't have to sell any dope for a while. Then I got this infection. I took medicine for it, but it wouldn't go away. My connection now was a guy named Ronnie. We were friends, and he was pretty good to me, giving me dope on credit while I had the infection so I wouldn't have to work, but after a few days he got fed up and told me I'd have to bring in some money. That night I went down with this guy who was unusually large—sexually that is—and the pain got so bad I could hardly walk. I was ready to faint. I took an extra shot of heroin so I could sleep, but when it wore off, I woke up crying. I went to Kings County Hospital. I hated to do it, because it would mean kicking my habit, and I was really strung out. But it wasn't too bad. I told them I was on drugs, and they gave me methadone. While you're on methadone, you don't get any withdrawal pains. They cleared the infection up, too, and I got out after a week. I went home, told my father I'd been in the hospital, and for once he acted real nice and understanding. I promised my mother I'd stop using drugs, and they said they'd be happy to have me live with them again. I meant it. I was fed up with everything. I really wanted to give up drugs, but I only lasted a day without them. I went over to see Charlotte. She and her boyfriend were shooting up, and that was all the encouragement I needed. In a few more days I was more strung out than I'd ever been before. Now it was Ronnie's turn to get busted. I was walking down Fifth Avenue in Brooklyn toward Lincoln Place when I saw him lined up against the wall with several other guys, the cops going over them. I just stood there and watched until they drove him away. Then I took a cab and went down to the precinct. I got there before Ronnie and the cops did. When they pulled up, I talked to the cops. They were detectives. They seemed like pretty good guys. I gave them a big sob story, about being a starving orphan or something—and they let Ronnie and me have lunch together with them before booking him. He gave me $200 he had on him. I promised to keep in touch. Then I went uptown in Brooklyn—uptown there means out east, up Fulton Street and Atlantic Avenue—and scored for $200 worth of stuff. Then I went downtown to my mother's house. It's hard for straight people to tell sometimes when an addict is taking dope. Especially when you don't want to believe it. You can act very normal, especially when you have a big habit. And by this time I was only shooting dope to feel normal. The more you're strung out, the harder it is to get a real strong high, even right after you've shot up. The way I'd get a real high then was sometimes to shoot cocaine along with the heroin. That goes right to your head and you feel out of this world, but it doesn't last. Sometimes I'd shoot cocaine before turning a trick. It would help turn me on.

"After Ronnie got busted, Charlotte and I tried to get off the street for a while. Whenever we scored, we'd try to sell half and shoot half ourselves. I was trying to keep Charlotte's habit down, not for any sentimental reasons, but so I'd have more stuff for myself. I'd always try to water down her shot. She'd squat on me to make sure she wasn't getting cheated, but I was very quick with my hands. Anyway, her habit wasn't nearly as bad as mine. She could still eat and keep food down. But not me. I was always nauseous, and I only weighed 119 pounds. But

I liked to be thin. I looked good. And I'd always hated being a fat girl."

Marilyn said that she never did get arrested during this period for hustling, although once she did pick up a cop who was in plain clothes: "He waited until I'd taken all my clothes off, and then he pulls out his badge and asks me if I ever fooled around with drugs. Of course I said no, and that I was only hustling because my mother was sick, and we didn't have enough money to pay the doctor. I don't think he believed me, but I was so young he let me go and told me to go home. He even insisted that I keep the money. I don't imagine there's too many cops like that, but there are some. As a matter of fact, whenever I ran into cops they were pretty nice to me. I guess I seemed sort of innocent."

Marilyn added that Charlotte had gotten busted once for prostitution but that it was one instance when she was innocent. "Charlotte and I were out together drinking all night," said Marilyn. "When the bars closed, Charlotte had to go to the bathroom. We didn't feel like walking over to Bickford's, and the trick house was around the corner. Charlotte just went in to use the toilet, but she picked a great time. It was right in the middle of a police raid. 'I was just here using the toilet!' she tells the cops. A likely story! So she spent the night in jail. As soon as the banks opened, we bailed her out, and had a real warm reunion. She was two years younger than me, and she was pretty scared."

One night Marilyn was out on the street, not trying to turn any tricks but waiting to meet Charlotte, when she struck up a conversation with a guy named Mickey who claimed to know Charlotte. He invited them both to come to his place, which they did, after scoring. He had a large hotel apartment and turned out to be a big dealer, although he didn't use drugs himself. Marilyn ended up sleeping with him, and Charlotte stayed, too, in the living room. Mickey didn't want any girl friend of his to be on dope—he hated it except as a business proposition—but he liked Marilyn and ended up leaving enough stuff around, when he went out to take care of her habit. She began living with him and was able to give up hustling on the street.

Around July 4 of that summer—1967—there was a sudden scarcity of heroin on the streets. Marilyn's habit was so big she resolved to try and kick on methadone—not to give up stuff forever—but to get her habit down to a practical size. She got hold of some methadone, but that afternoon around four o'clock Mickey came back. "He'd managed to score for a whole bundle," said Marilyn. "He asked me if I wanted any, and I said, no, I was doing all right on the methadone. Then at eight o'clock that night there was this banging on the door. It was the janitor hollering that he wanted to take away the dirty sheets. Mickey told him to go away and come back in the morning, but he kept on banging at the door."

At this point Mickey and Marilyn became suspicious. They hurried into the bathroom, tossed the bundle of stuff into a satchel, along with all the works, and heaved the satchel out the window. When they got to the door and unlocked it, two cops were waiting. "Luckily for him, Mickey acted real cool," said Marilyn. "Because the cops weren't after him at all. They were after Charlotte and me. And they had a warrant to take us away. My father had turned us in under the provisions of the Rockefeller program. There was nothing we could do about it. The cops were nice about it, as usual. 'Your father's putting you away,' was the way they explained it. At first I thought it might not be so bad—some kind of drying-out process like at Lexington. When the cops went on to explain that it was 'mandatory medical confinement' for three years, I was ready to kill my father. There was nothing to do but say good-bye to Mickey and go. He gave us each $5 for cigarettes and phone calls."

The cops took Marilyn and Charlotte down to the station house. The cops phoned their parents, but there was no answer. After a while Marilyn phoned her mother at work. She gave her hell and asked what did she think she and her father were trying to do to her? Her mother said she didn't quite understand what had happened, but that she was sure that what her father was doing was for their own good. In any case, the warrant was already out, and there was nothing anybody could do. Marilyn cursed her mother too and hung up. By this time both girls were feeling terrible. The cops gave them urine tests for heroin, and then some methadone. Then they were put in the infirmary.

It was two days before they had to show up in court to be certified. They were still on methadone and didn't feel too bad. When Marilyn saw her father, she spat on the ground. Her father told the judge that he wanted to put them away to save their lives—that he was afraid they were going to kill themselves.

Marilyn told the judge that she wanted to go to Synanon. The judge told her that anything like that would have to be worked out later. When Marilyn saw there was no practical way out of it for the time being, she kissed her mother good-bye, but she still wouldn't talk to her father.

The Rockefeller Rehab is at Tenth Avenue and Forty-first Street in Manhattan. "It wasn't so bad the first few days," Marilyn explained. "It was like a rest from all the tensions of the drug life. I mean it's bullshit that when you're on drugs you're drifting in some beautiful state of euphoria. Maybe you feel that way for half an hour after each fix. But the rest of the time you're hustling, one way or another. It's not quite as boring as a nine-to-five job, but the pressures are probably worse. I admit I had it relatively easy because I was young and I was living with guys I liked, first Warren and then Mickey, and I knew I could always go home if things got too bad, but the pressures of chaos were always there. It was nice to be off drugs, just lying around, bad-rapping with the other girls, and watching television. That's all we did. They had a school program, but it was optional. I slept whenever I could."

For Marilyn the sense of peace at being out of the street scene lasted for about one week. Then the boredom set in, and she'd never known what boredom was before. There were then about fifty girls in the Rehab, and after a week there wasn't anything at all to do, and there was the knowledge that things were going to go on this way for three more years. You'd get up and eat and rest and watch television and talk and go to sleep, and that was about it.

66

According to Marilyn, conditions in the Rockefeller program have not improved since she was in it. "It's worse now," she said. "A lot of the girls in Daytop now have been in the Rehab longer than I was. It was boring when I was there, but most of the girls were young like me and relatively innocent and hopeful. Most of them had been so naïve they'd turned themselves in voluntarily. They were mixed up. They thought that if you went in on your own, you could leave on your own, like at Lexington. Now the Rehabs are getting more of the older, hard-core addicts who feel it's a better deal than a long prison sentence.

"That Rockefeller Rehab! What a place after the first week! There was absolutely nothing to do except sleep, talk, and watch television. It was three weeks before my parents could even visit me on Sunday, when at least I could blow some steam off at my father. God, did I hate his guts for having me put away in that place! All the girls ever did was talk about breaking out. One night there was this enormous commotion. Everybody was yelling 'Fire!' and rushing this way and that. The halls were filled with smoke, and it was pandemonium. Police and firemen everywhere. When the smoke had cleared, it turned out that twenty girls had escaped. I was only depressed that I hadn't been in on the plot. And all the girls I'd enjoyed talking to had escaped. Now it was really depressing—without even good conversation. I decided to try and escape on my own, by climbing down a sheet outside the fourth story window. It could be opened with a nail file. I got a friend to distract the guard's attention. Then I tied one end of the sheet to a steam pipe, and climbed out on the windowsill, dragging the length of the sheet along with me. It was pretty scary out there, and I just let go for a few seconds, without climbing down, to test the strength of the sheet. I heard it start to tear and grabbed hold of the windowsill and climbed back in. I learned later that you were supposed to wet sheets to give them strength. A week later, another girl on the sixth floor tried the same trick. The sheets tore. She fell and was killed instantly. No one had told her about wetting the sheets either. For a while after that, no one messed around with sheets.

"Charlotte and I used to argue a lot, and one day the guards tried to separate us and put her on another floor. I told the guard to get the hell away from me. She backed off and went toward Charlotte. 'Don't touch her either, you bitch!' I yelled and hurled a bottle of Jergen's lotion at her. I knew that could get me into big trouble, so I broke down into tears and gave her a big sob story about how unhappy I was. And I promised not to get into any more fights. A few days later Charlotte and I got into a violent fist fight, and she was put on another floor.

"Now a new dimension of boredom set in. You had to have some routine, some little con game to keep yourself going. What I did was to tell the doctor that I was terribly nervous and unable to sleep, so I was given a pill every night. Instead of taking them, I hoarded them up. I don't even think they were barbiturates. Sometimes I thought I'd kill myself with them, and sometimes I thought I'd settle for one night of some half-ass high. In any case, one day when I saw my sister, she yells at me, 'Hey, Marilyn, how many of those pills you got by now?' Jesus. The guard was right there, so I rush back to my bunk and swallow the whole bunch of them—about twenty in all. Then I went into the bathroom and blacked out. When I came to, I was in the infirmary with a bad headache. I didn't get any more pills.

"I was going nuts. Myself and another girl decided to break out, employing the same tactics as those twenty girls. In the middle of the night we set our two mattresses on fire. But this time the guards were prepared. The exits were covered, and all that happened was that two guards were overcome by smoke and had to be hospitalized. The firemen came, and the whole place was a wreck. This girl and I denied everything, but they had a big formal investigation, and my name was mentioned twice. The reason the girls ratted on me was that the two officers hurt were the only decent ones in the place. They were more popular than I was. They claimed to have enough evidence to convict me of arson and destruction of state property. I was locked in a bathroom until morning and then taken down to police headquarters for fingerprinting.

"I'd heard how bad the Women's House of Detention was,

how it was filled with roaches and rats and bull dykes. I got there at three in the morning. They threw me into a cell and gave me five minutes to strip. Then they searched me, every inch of me, inside and out. They want to make sure you don't have any stuff hidden anywhere in your body. Those first few minutes I was there, as though right on cue, a huge rat ran across the cell, and I pulled the sheet open on my bed and there was a dead rat under it. I didn't sleep all night, but I did learn from a guard that my bail had been set at $1,500. I was allowed to phone my parents, and I said, 'Please, please, come down and bail me out.' The strange part of the whole situation was that the Rehab didn't know I could be bailed out of jail. In the morning I signed for my ring, my earrings, and, that afternoon, in court my parents were there. When I saw them, I promised to straighten out, but I was thinking about going back to Mickey. They bailed me out. I had on this funny-looking dress, so they bought me two new dresses and some sandals, and I stopped at a liquor store on my own and bought a couple of bottles of wine and drank one of them alone and the other with a friend. When I got home I covered my mouth so my mother wouldn't know I was drinking, and I asked Ann to walk around with me. I was thinking, I really put something over on them: I got into jail after setting fire to the Rehab and now I'm out of jail on bail and the Rehab doesn't even know.

"The next day I called up Mickey and went to see him. He'd been pretty nice, come to visit me often at the Rehab. He said he loved me and wanted to marry me. One day he came over to the house, and my parents liked him and told him he would be welcome there any time.

"The next day I copped. Mickey looked over my arms to make sure I wasn't shooting dope. But the marks didn't show yet. I only had a small habit, and I didn't want it to get out of control. I'd shoot, oh, three or four bags a day, but one night I found out from a friend that, while I was in the Rehab, Mickey had been seeing another girl. This made me feel bad and gave me an excuse to cop more dope. I got two bags from a guy who warned me that it was strong stuff and that I shouldn't shoot more than one bag at a time. But I don't know. I guess I really wanted to knock myself out. That stuff *was* strong. I OD'd and didn't wake up until noon the next day. It was the first time in my life that I'd OD'd. I found out that my friends had walked around with me for hours, throwing cold water on me to keep my circulation going, to keep me alive. It scared the hell out of me, but in typical dope-fiend fashion, it didn't occur to me to stop, just to be more careful."

Marilyn wanted to live with Mickey again, but, technically, she had to stay home because of the bail situation. She never did get a job and, finally, Mickey wised up to the fact that she was shooting dope again. He told her, 'Either cut me loose or cut out your habit. You can't cut down. You've just got to stop.' He was still dealing himself, but he didn't want the girl he lived with to be strung out on dope. He didn't like her that way, and it could endanger his operation. But Marilyn couldn't stop. She didn't want to stop, and Mickey left her. She began hanging out on Fourth Avenue again, hustling at night. She picked up with a guy named Tommy and his wife, Ellen, who'd hustle with her. She'd go to their place to shoot dope. She'd often stay with them the night. Ellen would call up Marilyn's mother, put on a good act and sound like she was a real responsible friend, fixing it up so Marilyn could stay out all night. It was during this time that Marilyn met a big-shot in the rackets who felt that she had a lot on the ball. He had this great proposition for her, since she was such a responsible person that people liked and that girls looked up to—he suggested that she open and operate a whorehouse up in the Bronx. They even had a site picked out, but Marilyn was too strung out by now to work out the details.

"It was during this period that I picked up a cocaine habit," she said. "I tried to shoot coke with every heroin fix. Now with coke you feel great for a matter of seconds, and then it's all over. That way the temptation is to keep shooting it again and again. Once I shot coke about fifteen times in two hours. It helped me turn on sexually."

The night before Marilyn's case came up again in court, she didn't get home until four A.M. She was high on coke and couldn't sleep. In the morning she told her parents she had to

70

go to the drugstore. Her idea was to go off and get a good fix before nine o'clock, when she'd agreed to meet her father at the drugstore. As he came around the corner, she was already nodding. Court was recessed when they got there, and her father took Marilyn to lunch. For once they were nice to each other. When court reconvened, the judge found out that Marilyn was supposed to be either in the Rehab or in jail. Bail was for going back to the Rehab, not for going home. That little game was over, so Marilyn told the judge, "Please don't put me in the Rehab. I'd much rather go to jail than back there."

The judge raised her bail to $2,500, over her father's objections, which meant that it was jail. "I went to the Women's House of Detention for seven days," said Marilyn. "Then my father came with the extra bail to transfer me back to the Rehab. Maybe he was ashamed to have a daughter in jail or maybe he thought the Rehab really would help. Anyway, he didn't want me in jail, so back I went to the Rehab.

"When I got back there, I had to admit that I'd been taking drugs again. It was obvious. There were tracks all over my arms, and I'd lost a lot of weight. But this time I felt different. I felt like doing something about myself. I had a counselor. She was nice, someone you could level with, and I'd heard by this time, not of Daytop specifically, but of places like it, and I asked her if she would help me get out of the Rockefeller Rehab and into a real rehabilitation program. It was a little tricky because I had these serious charges hanging over me: destroying state property, and arson in the second or third degree. These charges could amount to thirty years in jail. And now that I'd shot dope, I had to start the Rockefeller program all over again, and I was facing three years of that, even without jail. Things were looking bad. This counselor told me about Daytop and, a few days after, some girls from Daytop came to the Rehab to acquaint us with the program. It worked out that the day several girls went on probation to Daytop, including my sister, Charlotte, I was in court for a hearing, so I missed out. Charlotte wrote me from Daytop that she was very uptight there. She felt lonely, but she wasn't as lonely as me. I was crying every night. I'd write to Charlotte, tell her I hoped to see her there soon. In the meantime, I smuggled in some wine and liquor. We drank hair spray for a while, and then they wised up to that and stopped selling it in the commissary. One thing I did to pass time away was write letters to people in jails and other rehabs. I developed a huge chain of pen pals, people I'd never met. I had boxes and boxes of their letters. We'd compare what it felt like to be in jail, to be facing time locked up.

"Then one day I found I'd been accepted for an interview at Daytop. I never packed my bags so fast. It didn't mean I was accepted, but I had the feeling things were going to work out. All that bothered me was I'd been told that, if Daytop accepted me, I'd have to give up my letters, so I left them all with a friend at the Rehab. I used to wonder whatever happened to those letters. Now of course I've forgotten all about them!

"When I came into Daytop for my prospect interview—that was on March 12, 1968—I was given a rough time. I had to say I needed help, that I wanted to change. But they kept trying to make me cop to more than I felt was actually true. For instance, they spent a long time making me cop to how bad I felt having been a prostitute. I say this now, not just then: I didn't have any deep-seated guilt about it. I wasn't proud of it, but I didn't feel that bad about it. It was just something I had to do to make a living since I was on drugs. They kept at me, so I finally copped to the fact that I felt very guilty, because I realized that I wouldn't get in the house if I didn't. But the truth is that I felt worse about having stolen money from my mother. I also copped in the interview to being very slick and putting on a tough front so nothing could reach me. That was valid. Then they came out with this business of screaming for help. I said, 'I need help.' Then I smiled, and they said, 'What the fuck are you doing?' And somebody said, 'If you want to get in here, you'll have to scream so loud, you'll shatter the glass in that window.'

"And then they gave me this bit about my being out in the sea drowning, how this ship's going by for the last time, it's my last chance, and that's how loud I'm supposed to scream for help. Newspaper reporters pick up on that, and whenever there's a story about Daytop, someone's always quoted as saying that's the way they felt when they got into Daytop—they were going under for the third time, and then this boat came by. . . . They don't know it's a routine used in almost every prospect interview. So I screamed as loud as I could, and by the fourth time, I felt that I really did need help. At last they said, 'Okay. You're in.' My interview lasted two hours.

"I was very hostile during my first days at Daytop. I projected a real cool image, and whenever I felt uptight, I'd smile. I had a friend named Phyllis. She kept talking about splitting. A couple of days after I'd been there, they held a general meeting for people who were planning to split. I went in with this big smile on my face. I was protecting myself. The friendliness, the cheerful smile, was my bag. I had my first haircut the same day for being late to a medical trip, but even during the haircut, I was pretty well able to fend people off by being cool and humorous. This business went on with me a long time, and with it came another routine that had to do with my being or feeling that I was the laundress of the house, the black laundress. One of the assistant directors once asked me to iron two of his shirts. So I asked, 'Why should I iron these shirts?' I didn't like the idea. The coordinator said, 'You don't like ironing these shirts?' I said, 'No. I don't.' So they set up this haircut for me. A haircut is a vocal dressing down by older residents of the house. But in the haircut I betrayed myself. I didn't assert my real feelings. I said, 'Okay—I was wrong.' I began doing exactly what I was supposed to; just so people wouldn't bug me, to get them off my back. From then on, somebody'd say, 'Here's three shirts to iron.' And I'd say, 'Okay, just leave them there.'

"I made a commitment to lose weight. Since I'd been in the Rehab, my weight had gone up to 165 pounds. I lost a little weight, but losing weight has been my one colossal failure at Daytop. I could never quite make it, not really. Anyway, there was hardly anybody in the house who ever dumped me, who made a pull-up on me, who really challenged me. Everybody was buffaloed by my cool manner. I did what I was supposed to, and I was serving time. But that's about all. I wasn't relating to feelings inside me. I'd cut them all off so they couldn't hurt me. I felt like I was manipulating everybody, like a phony. And I didn't like feeling fat. After that haircut about not ironing the director's shirts, I did things like that for all the guys. I was ironing people's shirts, their pants, even their underwear, and I began feeling like a trick. One night a guy comes into my room and asks me to sew up a hole in the rear of his pants. Suddenly I said, 'Fuck this.' My friend Phyllis heard me, and she said, 'What's the matter?' And I broke down and told her that I felt like a trick in the house. I'd also had a lot of trinkets when I came to Daytop, and I'd given these away to the other girls, and I felt that I was buying friendship with them. So when this guy came around with his pants, I thought about it, and I said, 'No fucking good. I'm not sewing or mending or washing anybody's pants any more. That's it.' Then I went downstairs to the living room and burst into tears. There was this girl Ruth, who was black, and she was head of the women in Daytop. She later gave me this ruby ring. She left during the big split, but I looked up to her, and I was sitting there crying, feeling sorry for myself, when she came over and said, 'What are you doing? Do you enjoy sitting there having everybody watch you crying and making a fool of yourself? You got to build up what's strong and honest inside you, not carry on this way. Don't just go from feeling tough to feeling sorry for yourself. It's all the same trip. Start working on showing the real Marilyn.'

"That really pulled me up. It was the first time anybody'd said anything that helped me. I could see what she meant, how I'd go from one extreme to another in manner, still keeping my real feelings hidden. She made me feel good, and I said, 'You're right. Thanks. From now on I'm going to feel different.'

"She then explained to me, too, how it didn't help, just working very hard at your job, doing everything people tell you to, that you had to change inside. I'd been holding everything back. It was one thing to say, 'Yes. Yes. I'll fix your pants.' But then to feel bad about doing it. The thing was to talk about those feelings in groups, not just do things so people wouldn't attack you, which was the way I'd been operating at Daytop. So I had a good long cry, but there were no more pants fixed, not by Marilyn anyway.

"That was my first real change in Daytop, and I'd been there five months. After that I began to show real tears in groups, not just letting tears come because I thought they were expected of me. That's what I used to do—show a few tears now and then in between the smiles to keep them off me. I began to relate to other people's feelings. When a kid would start to split, I'd talk to him and keep him from splitting. I became active in groups myself, drawing people out. It was the first time I'd seen myself as the kind of person who could help other people, and this was a beautiful thing to realize, that I was someone other people liked to talk to and could trust.

"After that, I was in my first marathon. A marathon is a group that starts on Friday evening and lasts until Sunday afternoon with just a few hours off for sleep. You go into your past and into your feelings of anger, love, pain, and fear much more than in encounter groups. People who have been through marathons together get very close and never forget the experience. You let all your defenses down, and these beautiful feelings come through. You get into your whole past life, all your emotions, everything that's happened to you and hurt you. For the last year there hasn't been a single marathon at Daytop. Instead, they have probes, which are overnight groups that run about twelve hours. But they're usually structured to deal with some particular theme like homosexuality or prostitution. Anyway, my marathon was a beautiful experience. I began for the first time to relate to how I felt about my father, how hurt and angry I was at him, and I got into a kind of psychodrama where an older black fellow named Wilbur John played the role of my father. I found myself talking back to him in the old West Indian accent. He began to say, like my father used to, 'I don't want these black bitches in the house. Get them the fuck out of here!' Then, at the end, it was strange. He said, 'You know I love you, Marilyn! And I said, 'Forgive me, Daddy. Forgive me, Daddy.' I don't know. I began to realize that behind all the drinking and bad things he really did love me. It was then that I stopped hating him for the first time. Man, I came out of that marathon with this real groovy feeling, floating on air. I had other good experiences in the marathon. I felt very close to a guy named Paul from California. I cried for him, sharing how uptight he felt, having been in the Fort Worth program for years, and feeling every moment he had to prove himself. He was very rigid and controlled, and I felt it too. The fact was that I related to everybody. As soon as I stopped hating my father, it was like I was free, and everything became possible. I saw that he loved me in his own sick way. By the way, did I mention that he's stopped drinking? It happened a couple of months ago. I guess I must have a good influence on him—he'd been getting drunk every night for about twenty years. Starting a few months ago, I managed to talk to him about Daytop when he was sober, and he began to understand what I was doing. He took part in a couple of parents' groups, and suddenly he gave the whole thing up. One night, it was funny. I got my drinking privileges a few weeks ago. After you've been in the program about a year and a half, you're allowed to drink again, just socially, and one night I came home, and my father was up. I'd had a couple of beers, and my father smelled them on my breath, and he said, 'Have you been drinking, Marilyn?' 'All I had was two beers,' I said, and he said, 'You know what that can lead to. You know how I was for twenty years.' He looked very worried, like I was going to start drinking again, and I had to talk to him quite a while before he felt reassured enough to go back to sleep.

"After about six months, politics and sex began to enter my life at Daytop. The sex rites at Daytop are practically Victorian. As far as your first six months at Daytop go, forget it. After that, if you're responsible, and you meet someone you like and he likes you, you get permission to just sit down and talk together, away from the rest of the house. If things go good, you get permission to go to the movies with a chaperon, usually with another couple, and if things progress from there, you're allowed to go out to the movies alone together, and if you still show genuine love and concern and responsibility after a few months, you get permission to be alone and do whatever you want. But it's a long haul, and you have to be together several months before the final permission is given.

"In the summer of 1968 the retreat at Swan Lake was coming up. This is something we have every summer where the other two houses, from Fourteenth Street and Staten Island, get together at Swan Lake. It's supposed to be a communal vacation, but a lot of tensions build up. People feel displaced. There's over 300 people living together where there's room for about 100, and you end up with about six bunks in one room and separate work shifts, and everybody gets uptight. Two things were happening to me during this retreat. One was that this guy liked me a lot, and we told the directorship about it and we were together until he moved up into re-entry where you have to work for SPAN. SPAN stands for Special Project Against Narcotics. It's a neighborhood office on the Lower East Side of Manhattan where new kids are screened before coming to Daytop for their prospect interviews. It meant we'd be separated.

"I went to the retreat feeling bad about this. Then one night this young kid named Sammy—he's not black but Spanish—sits down and tells me he has eyes for me. I told him right off then, I said, 'I like you too, but I think of you as a friend, not as a boyfriend.' But Sammy ran me a long sob story about his troubles and how he liked me so much. Right then I should of said no to him and that's that, but I didn't, and I let the whole thing get started. In the meantime all this pressure was building up between certain staff members and David Deitch. They thought that David Deitch wanted to ultimately found a community for all kinds of radical ideas that could change America. They felt this wasn't a bad idea, but that a therapeutic community for drug addicts wasn't the right context for it. During the retreat I got into groups that David was running. He started a lot of black groups where we'd all rap about prejudice. This was good because there were relatively few blacks at Daytop and we needed to identify as a group, but I felt that something was phony, that this black group thing was being used for an ulterior purpose. At one of these groups, another black girl said that she didn't want to stay at Daytop and become part of a permanent community divorced from the outside world. I said I agreed with her and that I wasn't there to change the world. Then David said, 'What's wrong with bringing up your kids at Daytop?' I said, 'I don't want the feeling I'm going to live on Daytop property forever. I want to be independent once I'm straightened out.'

"Nothing got resolved during the retreat. People just went back to their different houses with all the tensions building up. For a couple of months things teetered along until the celebration of the founding of Daytop at Swan Lake. Now everything came to a head. Word got around that Dr. Casriel, the medical superintendent who founded Daytop, was planning to resign as a protest against David. In the end, the board of trustees had to decide which direction Daytop was going to take, and they decided for Dr. Casriel. Ronnie Brancato would be the new director. At our level everybody was divided into different groups saying, 'Come along with us.' I decided I would stay at Daytop whatever happened. Back at Fourteenth Street we were all so scared, we just performed the jobs we were assigned. For instance, I was assigned to clean the coffee urn. I took all day doing it just to keep the time going by so I wouldn't have to cope with these tensions. At one point someone gave me a $10 bill to go out and buy groceries with. It was the first time in months that I'd had $10 and I felt like splitting. But I didn't. I'd been there eight months now and I was almost a high roller in terms of seniority. I just hung tough.

"People were saying, 'Daytop is finished. This is the end. They're taking the egg and leaving the shell.' A lot of people made me feel like a traitor for not leaving. People who stayed were sent from Fourteenth Street to Staten Island for the night. Most of the black people were leaving, which made me feel bad. My sister Charlotte left too. When we got to Staten Island, a black named Tony, who I'd always respected and liked, was there. He was on the roadway in his car, trying to keep the Daytop cars from being driven off. People who were leaving were trying to take the files and records away, the cars, the food. A reporter had come from the *Staten Island Advance*. He talked

78

to both sides and nobody knew what was happening. This reporter came over to Tony, who had this steel bar from a jack in his hand. When the reporter questioned us, we tried to give the impression that there was no violence threatening, and Tony was trying to get this bar back into his car. He didn't realize the window was shut, so, as he talked to the reporter, he tried to toss it through the window, and this clank of steel on glass resounded. Tony got very uptight. It looked like the reporter felt that people were about to club each other over the head with jacks and clubs. Then a police car arrived with Dr. Casriel and Ronnie Brancato. People who were going, some of them, said to me, 'You little bitch, you're a traitor.' Then the people who stayed began to laugh, as though the whole thing was a big joke. The people who were going, they'd left the place in a filthy mess, food all over the place. It was like they'd been enjoying the whole crisis. I was the only female black person there, and during the next few days I began to feel like a maid again because I was black and everyone kept asking me to do all the dirty work. What was happening now was that Daytop was trying to survive the split. Immediately Ronnie Brancato, the new director, and Dr. Casriel were going to start building from scratch, and we began to interview new prospects for the house.

"It was during all this that I kind of accepted Sammy as a boyfriend. Because we'd both stayed, there was a bond between us and we saw a lot of each other. But I still had this feeling that I didn't like him as a man because he was smaller and younger than me.

"Now Tony was going back upstate to reopen Swan Lake, and he asked me if I'd like to go along and help him out. I said sure. Then Sammy got jealous because I was going up with Tony. At Swan Lake Tony pulled me into everything. He got me involved, and I really liked that guy. He was a strong person. He'd worked in the prison rehabilitation program. He gave me responsibility, and I felt involved. I was up at Swan Lake for about six weeks getting the new house going. Then I heard I was to be transferred back to Fourteenth Street. I was upset as though I'd failed. I said, 'What did I do wrong?' They said, 'Nothing. We need a woman now to go into SPAN and help out there. You're the best person we have.' But I felt sad because I felt close to everyone there. I didn't want to go to SPAN. At that time SPAN was just a neighborhood outpost where you took names and sent people to Daytop. Lonely. Now it's all different. SPAN has a whole program going where parents and neighborhood people participate. You can't even get into Daytop without going to SPAN first for two weeks. It's where you're supposed to kick your habit first. You go there every day and participate. But at that time it was just a clerical office where people signed up. You took people's names, you sent them to Daytop, and that was about it.

"When I left Swan Lake, a party was being set up for me. It happened to be my birthday, the same day I was leaving. I was trying to avoid everybody because I didn't want to say good-bye. I was feeling so sad. They gave me a mirror and on the card it said, 'When you're feeling down and you'd like to see somebody honest and good and beautiful, take a look at this.' That was a bit much. Then they gave me a cake and sang happy birthday. All I could say was that all the people that were there when I left, I sure hoped they'd all still be there when I went back. There were eighty-five people at Swan Lake then. I never did get to eat the cake. As it turned out, most of them were there when I went back to visit a few months later.

"It was while I was upstate, during that same period, that I finally broke up with Sammy. What happened was that he was after me continually. We'd been together so much that we'd reached the point where we could ask permission to go to bed together.

"When he came up one time for the weekend, this was what he had in mind. I felt something strange was going on. Usually, when your boyfriend comes to see you, you rush downstairs with open arms. But I didn't. In fact, I stayed up in my room all day. One of the assistant directors picked up on the situation and said, 'Something's wrong here. You'd better go down and have a special session and get it all straightened out.'

"So a special was called, and I came out with all the truth in that meeting. I'd been afraid of hurting Sammy, and because of that, I'd been carrying all this guilt around and feeling bad. I told him that he was too small, that he was younger than me, that I considered him a boy, not a man, that I didn't want to have any more to do with him, and that I was fed up with the whole business. Now that I wasn't feeling guilty any more, I was angry at him and at myself for having allowed him to impose on me that way. It was awful. I felt like I'd just been feeling sorry for him, and I told him so, and I told him to drop dead if he didn't like it. A lot of anger came out, and he just had to cope with it. I don't know how the hell he felt, but I'd never felt better. It was the first time I'd been honest about how I felt toward him. When we got to Fourteenth Street, we didn't speak to each other for a long time.

"I'd been back in Fourteenth Street a couple of weeks when one night I had to go to the bathroom. It was about two o'clock in the morning. I opened the door and there was a guy lying on the floor with blood all around him and a needle sticking out of his arm. It was a guy I knew well—I'll call him Billy—and he'd obviously taken an overdose. I woke up one of the coordinators. Dr. Casriel was called. They put Billy in the bathtub and filled it with cold water and worked over him for several hours until he came to. There was a big house meeting. Then Ronnie Brancato came over. He said the house was obviously in terrible shape and that everyone was going to have to take urine tests to see who'd been taking dope on the sly. He was really burned up. In fact, so was everybody. A couple of incidents like that are enough to get funds to Daytop cut off and the house itself closed down. Medical trips were set up, and everybody had to go to Staten Island. Two more guys split in the process. We had a general meeting for everybody planning to split. The urine tests turned everybody off. One girl was so uptight she couldn't even piss. We were filling her up with water all night so that she could take the urine test and go back to sleep, but she kept us all awake for hours before she was able to piss.

"All the tests came back negative

"I began working in the SPAN office, which I hated. Billy came back to Daytop, went to Swan Lake, and was thrown out again for shooting dope. All I did was interview prospects and send them to the house. I was just a clerk. There was no heat in the place. It was colder there than it was outside where there was at least some sunlight. We all had bad colds. It was so cold we could hardly write people's names down. We were just aching to get out of SPAN.

"When my tour of duty ended there, I was offered a part in the Daytop play, *The Concept*, as my second-stage job. Second stage at Daytop follows re-entry work at SPAN. It's where you go on living in the house, but have a regular job outside it. The play first opened a long time before the big split, and it's been running for over six months now since the reopening.

"Our director, Jacobina Caro, is a professional drama coach. But everybody in the play is an ex-addict. *The Concept* dramatizes everything we're trying to do at Daytop. Getting kids to stay off drugs is the end—but also just the beginning. It's a gradual process of humanization. Addicts are terrified of feelings and emotions, of their own and everybody else's. All we're really trying to do is to recognize and be in touch with our own humanity. *The Concept* dramatizes the day-by-day process through which this happens. Call it communal psychotherapy. The play shows a new prospect in his first interview, at morning meeting, then at afternoon seminar where he has to speak in public, in evening encounter groups, in a haircut, and in a marathon. Each of us has a "role," and we each play ourself in the role, drawing on our own experience so that, at best, the play becomes for each of us the ultimate way of baring ourselves before humanity—each night's audience. It's dynamite, it's so simple and direct, but it sure was scary when I started.

"I had to start my dramatic career from scratch. I didn't even know how to sit straight at first. It put us all through a lot of changes. We were in rehearsal for six months before we opened. Then we gave several one-night stands at Atlantic City, Philadelphia, Providence, and Trenton. And before we opened in

New York we had this chance to go out to California to stage the play for two weeks at Stanford and Los Angeles.

"When the day came to go to California, I packed in about ten minutes. I couldn't sleep all night. We left early in the morning. Going to the airport, getting on the plane, was such a groovy feeling, and I wished I'd never have to go back to Daytop. It was a rainy, cloudy day, but once we got up above the clouds it was all sunny and beautiful, and this great feeling of peace came over me. I felt I was really through with drugs, that I was only twenty-three, and that my whole life was just starting, and that I'd be through with Daytop, too, in a few months, and I'd be completely free, just the way I was feeling then, up above the clouds. I finally fell asleep.

"When I woke up, I was trying to be calm on the outside, but I was breathing so hard and fast at the prospect of arriving in California and putting on the play and everything. When we got to Palo Alto, we stayed in a kind of guest house just for people who were guests of Stanford University. Everybody had his own room. I really dug that privacy. There were two beds in each room, carpets on the floor, and I had the best room. I had something to say about that since I was head of the drama group! I loved every minute of it. The people there seemed so nice and warm.

"It was in Stanford that we experimented with a new ending for the play. After our enactment of the marathon scene in which we declare our need for love and our fear of it, it used to just end. We decided to open it up, instead, toward the audience. The whole cast would walk out toward the audience, following me, and for the last line of the play I'd cry out toward the audience, with my arms outstretched, 'Will you love me?' It was a beautiful idea, but it was pretty scary. I mean would they love me or would they panic and reject me? But it was worth trying. The first time I did it, my voice cracked, saying 'Will you love me?' I approached two women. One of them was crying, and she said, 'Yes,' and stood up and took me in her arms. This really turned the audience on, and soon each one of us was being embraced. It looked like the new ending for the play was a success.

"Then this woman who'd reached out to me said, 'Will you come over to our house to visit us? You're beautiful people and we'd like to see you.' Well, when this happens in New York, it's hopeless. I always suspect it's because I'm an ex-addict or because I'm black or because they think I'm an actress. It's not like they're asking you for real reasons, but I didn't feel like that with her. We went over that evening. I was scared. I wasn't used to being with older people. But we had a beautiful time. Her husband came home very late. He had a night job and he said when we left, 'Why don't you come out and spend the day tomorrow, and you can swim.' So we did that. They made us feel at home with them, very natural people. They took us driving up in the hills, and we saw the California countryside.

"Then we went to Los Angeles, to the University of California. We didn't get the guest house we were supposed to, and we had to stay in a hotel rather far from things, which made us dependent on a car, but again I had the best room with a kitchenette, TV, rugs on the floor, and there was a pool at the hotel, just like a resort, and I really loved having it, it had been so long since I'd had that kind of privacy, and we felt like real actors on a tour.

"They gave me a little pan to make my coffee in, and we could swim in the pool before we gave our performance. There was one funny incident, which wasn't so funny as it came out later. We'd gotten permission to go swimming late at night, after the pool was formally closed. And Phyllis and I—she was teaching me how to swim—one night we took the tops off our suits and left them at the side of the pool and went swimming that way. Nothing would have happened if we'd said nothing about it, but Phyllis mentioned it to somebody and by the time we got back to New York Ronnie Brancato called me into his office for a staff meeting. There was nothing but men there and he said, 'Well, I hear you girls like to swim in the nude.' I was so embarrassed, and then he really smoked us out. He brought out what could have happened if the papers had gotten hold of it. Ex-drug addicts swim naked in pool. Now if these headlines appeared in the paper, people could make it out that we were holding some sort of orgy. So, anyway, we felt sad to come back to Staten Island. It was a very beautiful experience that week, the way outside people responded to us, especially at Stanford. I cried when I got back. It was hard to fit back into the Daytop regime. For days I walked around without really participating in the house activities. There were new rules concerning the drama people. We had to go to at least three morning meetings a week, whereas before we had special privileges. And if we weren't at the meeting, we still had to be on the floor by ten. I felt very withdrawn and hurting inside. Nobody seemed to know it. We were alone and uptight. I'd go to sleep crying and wake up crying. And I was sick of being in groups with Sammy who was still feeling so much hostility toward me for not responding to him sexually. Finally in one group I got him to stop all that bullshit and, since then, it's been better.

"One day I changed my attitude. I'd been withdrawing, and I suddenly decided to go to all the morning meetings and I began to like it. It's as simple as that. You just decide to accept something, while if you fight it, it destroys you. I'd been going home for weekends a lot and something really beautiful had happened since my father had stopped drinking. Things were so different. My father would laugh at my mother, at the things she did, her crazy ways, instead of getting drunk and knocking her. One night my father told me, 'I feel proud of you.' I thought it was because we'd been on television, on the David Susskind show, but he'd missed that. It was typical of my family that they would forget about it, or not bother to turn it on. It was a beautiful program, two full hours of talking to the cast of the play.

"After that, it was strange, people who had seen me on TV would stop me on the street and ask me for my autograph as though I were a movie star. But when my father said, 'I'm so happy that God blessed me with a child like you,' he hadn't even seen that program. He was just feeling good. Missing the program was my older sister Ann's fault. I told only her about the TV show so it would be a surprise for my parents, but she fell asleep and forgot to tell them. My mother was crying, but she didn't give a damn about missing the David Susskind show. She was happy my father was dancing with her and we were home to see it.

"It's a strange thing, to go home, especially when I walk through the old neighborhoods where I used to hustle, like on Fourth Avenue. One day I saw this woman; she was a girl, but she looked like an old woman. She'd left Daytop during the big split, and I ran into her in the street and I stopped her. She didn't want to talk to me, but she told me that she was using dope again, and she had these huge dents in her arms, not just from heroin, but from shooting a procaine synthetic. It burns all the skin away, and she had abscesses on both her arms, and she was with this bogus-looking guy, and she told me that she was happy for me, but that she would rather kill herself than go off drugs and have to face normal life.

"Meanwhile, the play was going good. You'd think when you're all together on it, it would come off better, but that's not true. One night, for instance, no one felt like doing it at all. We were just trying to get it over with, yet it came out as one of our best performances and everyone commented on it. The thing is that when you're really feeling good and everyone says, 'Let's push for some kind of standing ovation,' well, you're together so much that you can block the audience out. Sometimes we'd have terrible fights when everybody was against each other. I was the leader of the drama group, and I was often mad at everybody. To begin with, I was pissed off about one scene about prejudice. I explain to the white guy how he's prejudiced against blacks. We never have a scene where blacks are prejudiced against whites. The whole premise of the thing made me angry, and I sulked and refused to do the scene. And that hurt everybody, once my discipline was off. And I got mad at Sammy, who was in the play, and he told me I was goofing off, and I called him an inch. I told him he was a tiny little guy that weighed half what I did. How could I possibly want to go to bed with a guy like that? And Phyllis attacked Dave for talking too much, somebody accused Ralph of being a total blank. Phyllis attacked Dave again for having a sunken chest, for acting like a fairy, and he was so angry his whole face was distorted and he looked like he was going to have a heart attack. And he told Phyllis she looked like a man, and all this time the audience thought it was part of the play, and they were lapping it up. Well, why not? It was part of the play that night.

"What hurts me most at Daytop these days is when someone I'm close to splits. Like old Wilbur John, the guy who helped me, playing my father in the marathon. He was black and thirty-nine years old. He'd been in the house eight months, and one day he was in a car on a medical trip with some girls and he opened his pants and just pee'd all over the place. He was thrown out of Daytop for good. It's so crazy. Some say that older people are easier to treat in Daytop because they've had enough of the street. It's not true. I figure Wilbur John couldn't face splitting, but he wanted out, so he just did something completely far out that was as good as his death warrant, and behind his old fears he was a beautiful guy. I say older dope fiends need more love than the young kids. Ninety percent of the people in Daytop are around twenty or twenty-one, so it's harder when you get up around thirty-eight or thirty-nine. You can't fit in, and you need a great deal of support and love from the rest of the house. Wilbur John had been in jail for ten years. If they get him now, he could go back to the joint for the rest of his life. I hear he's in the Tombs, but nobody knows anything for sure, except that he won't be back in Daytop. This was a guy that a lot of people really dug when he was here. Oh, it's tough when older guys split. Especially people who have become coordinators or something. If you leave Daytop and you come back, and you've been giving people data and telling them how to act, you feel like you have to face all these people again, and it's really very hard. It takes an enormous amount of guts to come back from splitting after you've become a coordinator like Greg did. Most of them try to get in some other program. That's the easiest way to do it, because you have so much guilt in you from being in one house and having helped people, and you feel like a phony, and the best way, I think, is simply to start over, somewhere else. A lot of people ask me how I'll feel if I ever choose a man to live with or marry. Do I think it would be best if he were an ex-dope fiend too? My feeling is no. I'm so sick of dope, so sick of the whole scene that I'd rather meet someone who never heard of dope, never had anything to do with it.

"I just saw Warren again. He's off dope. He went from jail to Phoenix House and got himself all straightened out, and he told me he was still in love with me. I always had good feelings for him, but I had to say no. That's over.

"Someday I'd like to have a job that has nothing to do with addicts. I mean, I'm only twenty-three, and I'm starting my life. I want to mix with people who have other problems. As far as the concept goes, there are two things I think: there's willpower and there's patience, but patience is more important because willpower can be phony. You can will yourself to do things all right, but it can tighten you up and get you out of touch with your feelings. But if something unpleasant happens and you feel like splitting or shooting dope, you just hang tough and tell yourself to wait twenty-four hours, and then see how you feel. That seems to work better. It's always tough here. It's not like you have a choice. You *have* to hang tough.

"You just take things slowly, and it's the small things that matter. When we were shooting dope, big things seemed so important. That's one of the queer things about it. I was full of ideas, big wishes, big frustrations. But we didn't have anything to do with people really, not in the small ways. We were like vegetables with big dreams. We weren't doing anything. We were even scared of getting angry. We were scared of the smallest wishes even. Like I used to wear dungarees. I would never wear a dress. I couldn't understand how my sisters liked to wear dresses. I didn't even want to wear high-heeled shoes. I always wore flats. Now I wear heels. I didn't have the guts then to know what I wanted to do. It was like I couldn't compete with other women, I guess. If I ever had a dress on, people would say, 'Where are you going? What's the occasion?' But nobody could make me wear dresses until I wanted to. Now I'm wearing dresses. I dig them. My mother's happy about it, too. When I'd go home before, even from Daytop, after I was pretty well fixed up, I'd still bring home my dungarees. I thought Charlotte was crazy for buying shoes. Now I'm strung out on buying shoes and dresses. My favorite thing to spend money on now is shoes and dresses. But it's not the shoes and dresses exactly. It's like you suddenly go back to simple things you never felt before. And you start from there. Where you feel things. Where you have wishes. It's so different from the old way. How I used to hate myself, my hair, my freckles, my fatness! But now I love Marilyn!"

Paul

"OF COURSE I don't think of it that way now. But until I got busted I was pretty lucky. I come from Lancaster, California, a town about forty miles north of Los Angeles in the Mojave Desert, and I always loved the country out there. Unlike so many junkies, I was never part of any dreary ghetto scene. I never even had much to do with any big cities except to go there to score, ball chicks, or, more important, make a sale. Although it's lunacy to describe being strung out on heroin in any terms of success, I was living pretty high off the hog until I got busted. You could say that I managed to realize the great American dream of every junkie out there—at least for six months. I had a beautiful setup, all the money I needed and all the junk I could use—just for driving down to Mexico three times a week and making one connection. And this we pulled off without any of the hassle you get into if you're mixed up with the syndicate. Me and my two buddies, we were independent. I could make a phone call right now and be back in business making over $1,000 a week. It's a crazy claim for a senior coordinator at Daytop to make, but I used to think about it sometimes when I was first in the house. After being locked up in the joint for three years, you think of every possibility.

"As far as childhood is concerned, I had the same kind of screwed-up background that most addicts had. Not that I tried to put the blame there, even after I came to Daytop. I tended to be dishonest in just the opposite way. I thought of myself as being above all that kind of Freudian stuff, too big and independent a guy to be hurt, say, by the way my father made me feel that I'd let him down. It was a long time before I could relate to that pain. Even when I was fourteen and my father walked out on us all, I tended to blame my mother. It was always me who was supposed to have let *him* down.

"I was born in 1939, and until 1946 my father was away in the war, and I lived in Los Angeles with my mother where she worked in a factory. I started off in Catholic grammar school. My mother was a devout Catholic of German background, but my father's people, of Scotch-Irish extraction, had been Christian Scientists. They were both good-looking, but my father was shorter than my mother, and I think he must have always had a complex about being small.

"When my father returned from the war in 1946, he had a Purple Heart for being wounded in the Pacific. We moved out to Lancaster again, bought a new house, and my father went back into the upholstery business, which my grandfather had founded there in 1925. The land our house was on used to be desert. It was cut up into tracts—what you call lots here in the East—but there was more space there—a hundred and twenty-five feet of grass on our tract. And Lancaster wasn't like either a small town or suburbia. There were elm trees on the road, but no sidewalks, lots of greenery and flowers, and a wind that smelled of the country. The population then was less than 15,000, though today it must be more like 50,000. And two or three miles out, you ran into real open land.

"I started going to public school, and every afternoon after school I had to go down to my father's shop and strip chairs. I was good at the job, but I hated it. I couldn't conceive of more boring work. My father was restless and impatient with everything I tried to do. I never lived up to his expectations. I was active in sports, and my father bought me a new baseball glove which soon got stolen. Instead of feeling bad about it, as I did, or maybe even offering to replace it, he behaved as though it were my fault, as though I were supposed to track the culprit down, like a detective. When I went to camp in the summer, he came out to visit me, and one day I was diving into the water for these white rocks that were seven feet deep. The water was ice-cold, it was hard for me to hold my breath, and I couldn't come up with any of the rocks. My father treated me as though I were some kind of coward or failure. This restlessness in him got worse. He had a pilot's license, and he bought a Piper Cub which he used to go flying off in. He only took me up in it twice—kidding me about how nervous I was—before he cracked it up. He was drinking a lot. He'd arrange these expeditions that always started off in a serious manner but would end up in a chaos of disappointment and bad feeling. On my twelfth birthday he gave me a shotgun, and we went out into the desert to hunt and look for semiprecious stones. I liked the outdoors, but when I went with him, it always ended up badly. He blamed me for not having the true pioneering spirit and for being soft and spoiled. I see now it was all projection from his own self-doubts. He was always talking about courage and stamina and aggressiveness, yet when we were home and a simple problem came up, like my wanting to go to the movies, I'd ask him, and he'd say, 'Go ask your mother.' On the other hand, when I went to her, she'd say, 'Go ask your father.' One Sunday we were having watermelon. My father was slicing it up. The knife slipped, and he cut his thumb, which began to bleed like hell. When I saw the blood, I started to cry and ran out of the room. For days afterward my father chided me about this incident, saying that I was chicken and would always be the first person to hide under the table when a crisis came up.

"I had a brother nine years younger than me, and a sister twelve years younger. When I was fourteen years old, my father took me aside and said, 'I'm leaving. You're the man of the family now. What happens here is your responsibility.' With that, he walked out of the house, and none of us ever heard from him again. We don't know where he went or what happened to him."

Because there had been so much bad feeling between them, his father's departure was a relief to Paul. But it left him with a feeling of emptiness, too. His father's upholstery business had failed, and his mother went to work as a waitress—a line of work she stayed with for the next fifteen years. Because there were three children in the family, and his mother didn't earn much, they qualified for welfare; Paul worked as a waiter after school. Just before graduation he quit high school, his rationale being that he had to go to work full time to help support the family. He was eighteen, which disqualified them from further state aid.

Until that year, Paul had been active in athletics. During his junior year he had pitched regularly for the baseball team, but when he went out for football the next fall the doctor found that he had a hernia. Paul went to the county hospital in Los Angeles for a hernia operation, and the doctors there found that he had a heart murmur. Instead of being able to play football, he was put in a corrective gym class. "I didn't sit around stewing for long about the loss of my athletic career," he said. "Instead I looked around to see what else was happening, and the whole pot scene appealed to my expanding horizons. I had a role model too. An older kid I looked up to, who'd been a big athlete, suddenly dropped out of school, took a part-time job, and began driving around the countryside, smoking pot and partying, and his style of life had a great appeal to me. In fact, my first taste of pot was all mixed up with my feelings for nature and the wide open spaces. Anywhere you drove out of Lancaster it was beautiful. West, you'd go through the alfalfa fields and into the mountains. Driving south, you'd go through orchards of apricots, peaches, and plums. East was the Mojave Desert. North were almond trees, rolling hills full of juniper, then the wheat fields descending into Antelope Valley. Up in the hills, you could see for fifty miles in every directon. There were red and orange poppies, acre after acre. You'd drive through there, hit a patch of desert, and after that would come the scent of alfalfa. Lake Hughes was in the west, and every Sunday we'd drive out there with girls. We had a castle to live in every weekend at Lake Hughes—an abandoned castle we'd taken over as our own. It was surrounded by huge cherry trees we parked our cars under, and when we left late Sunday night our arms were full of these huge ripe cherries. No matter how hot it got in the day, a wind would come up in the afternoon, the leaves blowing all around us, and at night it would go down to about seventy. Pot was cheap out there. When we wanted it, we would drive to Redondo Beach and pick up a kilo for about $60. It came in a tight block, and we'd make thirty-six one-ounce cans and sell them for $10 an ounce. After keeping what we wanted for ourselves, we'd come out with a profit of $200.

"There was a whole crowd of guys who'd dropped out of the athletic scene for something they liked better. We had the same backgrounds, although most of these guys' parents had more money than mine ever did. They were upper middle class, came from good homes, and had cars to drive around in. Cars out West were an essential part of the drug scene—both for dealing and enjoying the stuff ourselves. For several months I had a job in a training program at an aircraft company. What I liked best about the job was sitting around the airstrip after work with a couple of buddies, smoking pot and popping pills, and listening to the roar of the jets coming in. From the start, pot was a source of income as well as pleasure. Dealing, though, was sporadic. There was no real system. When I needed cash I burglarized vending machines and small stores and offices. I'd first been arrested for breaking and entry when I was fifteen and had gotten off on probation. Since then, I'd become more cautious or liked to think so. At least I didn't go around boasting about these escapades. We kept going out to the castle in Lake Hughes, and there were always plenty of girls who were willing to go with us. At this point we were popular. The more straight people seemed to get a kick out of us, and we were invited to the lush parties. Our pattern was to hang out at these parties early in the evening, getting primed up on liquor, and then take off around midnight to start pot parties that kept going all night. If it was Friday night, they'd go on all weekend, and sometimes into Monday. Those who were still in school just wouldn't show. Those who had jobs would call in sick. If any of the parents were on vacation, we'd take over their house while they were away, throwing parties and sleeping all day. Somebody was

95

always driving somewhere in those days, and I was always going along for the ride. We were happy. It seemed like this style of life could go on forever, that nothing bad would happen to us. And when the cops began to get onto us, we didn't take it too seriously. For those of us who'd gotten arrested, there always seemed a way out. Parents would come down and put up bail. Cases would be postponed. We felt we'd be protected from anything bad that would happen. But we were careful, especially when we were dealing in pot. One morning though, we sold some pot and pills to a kid we knew for $46. He was in the Marines, and we didn't know that he'd been busted the night before for selling. Scared of getting court-martialed, he agreed to cooperate with the cops, and the money he paid us was marked. The next day we heard how this kid had ratted on us. I went to Los Angeles for a few days, hoping it would all blow over. But when I got home I was arrested. That guy in the Marines had given the police no less than thirty names, which covered just about the whole crowd I ran with. He'd particularly implicated me and my best friend, Jack, in the $46 sale of that pot. I was charged with sale, Jack with possession. Jack's parents got us both out on bail for a total of $2,500. There was an $800 lawyer's bill. Our cases were postponed for five months, so we still had the summer ahead of us. When my mother learned what had happened, she was really angry and gave me a last warning: no more pot, or else. I said okay. When, just a few days later, she found some joints I'd left right on the bed after changing my clothes, she threw me out of the house. I moved in with some friends. The pot parties went on, though we exercised more caution. We were lucky too. One night we were throwing this party, and we had four kilos of pot. We had one kid keeping an eye out for cops. Sure enough, about one in the morning, three cop cars descended on the scene, but this kid warned us in time, and about twenty-five out of thirty of us hid upstairs in an attic. Five of the kids were picked up and questioned, but they didn't talk, so the cops had nothing on us. We got away with a lot that summer."

In the fall Paul's case came up and he was convicted of selling marijuana. The concrete evidence of the marked bills, combined

96

with the testimony of his stool-pigeon friend, was too much for his lawyer. Paul was sentenced to fourteen months at the Youth Authority of Soledad State Prison. He was nineteen. He was put in the North Facility, an experimental project with supposed advantages over the rest of the penitentiary. There were 600 prisoners in the North Facility—compared to about 3,000 in the central prison. But conditions were the same as in the main prison except for some improvements in the physical facilities. There was a gymnasium, a library, classrooms, and two recreation yards, but, according to Paul, this made no real difference. "There was wholesale selling of bodies when young kids came in who didn't know how to handle themselves. Older guys worked in the kitchen, and when the younger guys were sent in there to help out, cleaning up trays and mopping up, they'd be looked over and it was decided who would get first crack at whom sexually. I was big for my age and could handle myself well, and I made it clear that no one was going to mess around with me, despite my age. And they didn't. There was intense hostility between the guards and the inmates, even more between the black and Spanish-speaking prisoners, who were at each others' throats all the time. One night the tension had been building up during supper at the chow hall. Everybody was scared, especially the guards. It was Saturday, and later that night a movie was shown on a screen in the gymnasium. In one sequence a riot broke out within the movie, and this touched off a real riot in the gymnasium. Absolutely all hell broke loose. The blacks and the Spanish were tearing each other apart, and even the hacks were fighting to get out of the room. When it was finally broken up, 150 of them were sent to San Quentin."

With time off for good behavior, Paul completed his sentence in nine months, and went back to Lancaster. After his stretch in prison, Paul was eager to pick up again where he had left off. But of the Lancaster crowd he'd gone with, most were either in jail or had moved away to Los Angeles and San Francisco. Paul had no money and no car and was staying with his mother. Eventually he ran into one old friend who agreed to drive him to Redondo Beach, where he had arranged by telephone to meet a girl he knew. It turned out that the friend had scored on heroin just before starting out and was nodding at the wheel through-out most of the trip, but they made it. Paul picked up the girl and they went to the beach and smoked some marijuana. Suddenly something horrible happened to him. "I didn't know if it was the heart murmur kicking up again, or my nerves, or the pot," said Paul, "but I felt like my heart had stopped beating. I washed my face in the ocean, but it didn't help. My chest was constricted and I could hardly breathe. This girl gave me three Seconals, and in about twenty minutes I began breathing again, and the pressure left my chest. I felt relaxed and good. The Seconals had fixed me up, and I proceeded with the business at hand, which was getting the girl and myself into bed."

In the days ahead Paul succeeded in tracking down some of his other friends who had left Lancaster, and found that they weren't partying any more in the old lighthearted way. Their lives had changed since Paul had been in prison. Some of the boys had gotten married and others had taken jobs. None was still being supported by affluent parents. But those who had jobs were bored and were just waiting for the opportunity to do something different.

Paul found six of them living in a house on the East Side of Los Angeles. There they had three five-gallon containers—full of sleeping pills, amphetamines, Dilaudid, Demerol, and morphine. They went to their jobs every day, but spent their free time popping pills and plotting a bold counterfeiting operation. Using a $400 camera and silk-screen printing equipment they had obtained, they intended to manufacture $100 travelers' checks. The prints for the patterns and serial numbers of the checks had already been stolen. They planned to distribute about $50,000 worth of these checks for 500 miles in every direction. They would distribute them intensively—but only for one week, before anyone could even discover that they were bogus. This time limit was to be the secret of the scheme's success. If any checks were left after that week, they would be destroyed along with all the equipment. They would split up the profits, then leave the country separately to live either in Mexico or Europe. "The scheme appealed to me," said Paul. "But I was terrified of going back to prison on some enormous sentence. Even five years seemed impossible to consider. I ended up humoring these guys, pretending to go along with them, but vaguely hoping that my commitment would not be put to the test. All I really wanted was some money, a car, and a girl, and the leisure to get high. Because of this pending project, these guys had gotten what they considered to be very careful and clever in matters of transportation. They would only use their own cars when it was a question of driving down to the supermarket to buy some groceries. When it came to needing transportation for pot and pills, they had a whole other racket going. What they'd do—or rather what we'd do, since I was into it too—was to buy a junked car, take the serial number off it, then steal a working car of the same year and model, replacing its serial number with the one we'd bought. This scheme worked fine for a while. Of course it never occurred to these guys to stop using drugs until they'd pulled off the counterfeiting plot. That would have been too simple. What we didn't know was that the cops were watching us just for our traffic in pot and pills. One night we were driving from the city out to the beach. We had ten pounds of pot with us and a hundred bottles of pills we were going to sell. The pills had been stolen from a drugstore, but the cops didn't know about that. When the cops picked up our trail, we tried to shake them off, but they got nearer. We pulled onto a dirt road off the main highway, but this didn't fool them, and when we saw that they were within a hundred yards of overtaking us, with great reluctance we hurled all the pills and the pot out the window. The police tried to ram us, but, instead, they ran off the road and we got away. We speeded up, but the car hit a bump which dislodged the throttle valve, and we came to a halt. The police got us. Although we'd thrown the stuff away and there was no evidence, they were so angry about the chase that they beat the shit out of us and took us down to the station house. They said that whatever happened to us because of this escapade, they'd be watching us from now on, with tanks and submarines if necessary, and that we wouldn't have a chance. We wouldn't be able to move around there any more. Although we didn't have any pot on us, they searched our pockets, and in some cases found minute particles of it. I got off. My pockets were clean. But three of them got sentences of sixty days. This put an end to the counterfeiting project, and I was somewhat relieved.

"In the meantime I'd been making it with this girl and she got pregnant. This was a total nightmare. It was almost as bad as facing jail. She was scared too. We went to a doctor and got quinine pills. She took mustard baths. I went running with her up and down the beach. But nothing worked. She was pregnant, and she was only sixteen. Three weeks later we got married—an occasion I celebrated by taking a fix of heroin outside the church. I was taking heroin at this time only for occasional kicks. A week after our wedding she had a miscarriage. We were both so relieved that we began to really dig each other. It was nice. I liked her, and within six months she was pregnant again. This time we decided to go ahead and have the baby, even though I was still scared of the responsibility. We moved from Los Angeles to Burbank and settled down in a fabulous apartment. I was still messing around with drugs on weekends, but it was cool."

From the training program at the aircraft company, Paul had enough experience to qualify for a job with an electronics firm outside of Burbank. He was taken on as a trainee. The firm specialized in the construction of circuit boards for computers. Paul's immediate superior—who helped him get the job—was an older addict. They formed a close relationship on the basis of their work and mutual interest in drugs. The work involved the use of valuable materials: gold, silver, copper, platinum, cobalt. It wasn't difficult for them to steal about $200 worth of these substances a week. Paul was earning a good wage too, $180 a week without overtime, and his wife had a job that brought in an additional $90 a week.

"This apartment we had was fabulous," says Paul. "You get away from the coast in California and the rents really drop. In Burbank for just $115 a month, we had a beautiful brand-new apartment with bay windows, huge walk-in closets, two bedrooms, with complete air-conditioning. And the bathroom! When you climbed out of the tub, an automatic radiant dryer went to work on you. Piped in music came out of the walls. And outside there was a swimming pool shared with other tenants living in the complex. It was more like a country club than an apartment house. We gave parties, and for the first time since I'd been out of prison I felt that the police were off my back.

"A remarkable thing in our marriage was that my wife didn't know I was involved with drugs in any way. But my boss and I were having a hell of a time together. The work we did was extremely delicate and sensitive, and we managed to do it very well. What we'd do, though, was stay late at night, when our work was done, getting bombed out of our minds, while we drew overtime for it. It was quite a setup. Nor were we always alone on these late shifts. One night, for instance, one of my boss's friends arrived with six jars of pills—1,000 pills in each jar. There was everything there: pain pills, Demerol, yellow jackets, Dexadrine, morphine. One bottle contained 1,000 half-grain tablets of morphine. It was very high-quality stuff. This guy was a friend. He'd picked it up practically for free, and he sold us the whole lot of bottles for $25. That's how easy it was for us to score. The stuff was everywhere, and guys who knew each other enjoyed being generous with each other. It was kicks. We also used it generously. I remember that two weeks after we'd gotten that bottle of morphine, we'd shot half of it. We'd sometimes stay in the shop as late as three in the morning, just getting high and rapping. The only thing we didn't do there was bring girls in.

"I was really feeling good—on top of the world. I had a promising job that I was good at and liked. It looked as though I was cut out to become a specialist in electrochemistry—a field that was opening up in every direction. Even though I was using a lot of dope, it wasn't affecting my work. I was having a great time, getting high when I wasn't working. And my wife was pleased with me and had no idea that I was becoming a dope fiend. I tried to confine that side of my life to after-hours in the shop. In 1962 we took a beautiful vacation together for two weeks. We drove to San Francisco in seven hours. I took along in my suitcase 1,000 Benzedrine pills and a kilo of pot. When we got to San Francisco, I linked up with some old buddies that had moved there from Lancaster. One friend was married to a Playboy Club bunny. After my wife was asleep at the hotel, we met and he said, 'You want to score on stuff?' I said, 'Okay,' and we got high on methedrine. Then we went to the black section where we scored on heroin. The stuff was so good it drowned out the methedrine. These guys in San Francisco all had jobs too and were doing well. They were taking speed and heroin on weekends for kicks, but without apparent consequences. It didn't seem like anybody was going down hill. It was the equivalent of the alcohol people getting drunk after work and on weekends.

"As my drug habit began to increase in frequency and scope to include more hard stuff, I didn't give it a thought. I felt I could handle anything. Basically, I was very ambitious, and it was as though I were exercising my ambition as much on dope as on my work in the shop. They seemed to go together. The harder I worked, the more dope I felt entitled to use as recreation. Consequently, I began to act a little crazy. This was about the time that my son was born. One Friday night I got a phone call. A friend of mine had two girls with him. I told my wife I was going out to get the paper, and I didn't come back for three days. We went to Palmdale to one of the girl's apartments and stayed there overnight. The girl I was with had a prescription for morphine, and the next day we decided to use it, but she wanted to find a druggist outside her home territory. We drove all around the countryside and wound up in a town near Lancaster, where I had had some dealings with the local druggist. There we were, waiting for the prescription to be filled, when in the door walks this narcotics officer who'd helped send me up to Soledad Prison. He recognized me immediately and said, 'What the hell are you doing here?' I was already high on pot, and I was scared that he'd pull me in. I was feeling vulnerable and guilty. But just then a squad car pulled up. There was some kind of crisis, and another cop called to this guy, 'Hurry up. They need you.' They all drove off. I knew it was a close call and that he would have arrested me on some charge or other. In fact behind the surface of my life now, a new tension was building up. When that narcotics officer came into the drugstore, I was really terrified, though I pretended to laugh it off and resumed what I considered to be my charmed life. For that instant, all my good feelings were obliterated, and I felt inside that I was on the verge of a catastrophe.

"This feeling of terror arose on other occasions. One evening, for instance, I was with a friend driving a dump truck out in the desert. We were smoking pot. Life was cool and beautiful. Then suddenly the car was shaking furiously. We heard a terrible racket, wind blowing all around us. It was a police helicopter that was on our trail. We hurled all the pot out the window. The police landed. They found nothing on us, and we were allowed to go on. But it was another close call that made me very aware of how shaky our defenses really were.

"Another night, with another friend, we were driving through fields of alfalfa. We'd been smoking and had two cans of pot with us. It was very late, and we were far from the usual territory covered by any city or state police. I didn't feel threatened by anything. There was a sweet smell in the air, and the moon was out. We were driving slowly, to take it all in. Suddenly, in the headlights, I saw these eyes on the side of the road. My friend was driving. I said, 'My God! What the hell is that?' He almost swerved off the road and said, 'What? What do you mean?' I said, 'There's some eyes out there!' And before we could get a grip on ourselves, this enormous jackrabbit leaped across the hood of the car. I was convinced it was a cop or something. My friend jammed on the brakes, almost cracking the car up. Just after he jumped, we hurled the two cans of pot out the window. Even after we knew it was a rabbit, we swept out the whole car in case there was any trace of weed on the floor.

"This whole pot thing when the cops are after you can get you paranoid. It's so easy to plant the stuff or to find a trace of it, a little dust on a rug. I never heard of a cop going into a vacuum cleaner to find particles of pot, but it's the kind of thing that they would do, and it occurred to me because I used a vacuum cleaner to clean out my own car. In fact I did this the morning after the jackrabbit incident. It was better when you were out in the open spaces, like the night the police helicopter descended on us. The cops didn't have a chance. The stuff blows away in the wind, and the desert's as good as the sea. But when

103

you're indoors, it's hard stuff to get rid of in a hurry. And we'd always have so much of it around. There'd be a few cans, and what do you do with a few cans of pot? It's hard to even flush down the toilet because it floats. And there's usually traces of it somewhere.

"Anyway, this feeling often stayed with me; it would sneak up on me at odd moments, and the best way to get rid of it was to take more dope. It was at this point that I got more and more into heroin. It made me feel secure again. It was the ultimate weapon for blocking out pain and fear of any kind. This line was very thin. You'd be feeling terrific one moment, and some little thing would happen, and you'd be saying, 'My God. I'm about to go to jail. I'm about to be exposed.' I think that was the feeling: *They're about to see me for what I am. They're about to get me!*

"The police had our number, and their raids became more frequent. We began to expect them to show up, and if we were high enough, we'd actually try to block out their physical presence. This wasn't a bad tactic the first time. At least it was an original approach that disarmed them. One night there were just a few of us. We were full of pills, but the source was well hidden. We'd been smoking pot, but it was all used up. We were just coasting along, nursing our highs safely with a keg of beer, and feeling very secure. The cops pulled up slowly with their car lights off, and they even had an assistant DA with them. They must have figured they had us over a barrel. Instead, when they broke in, we were just sitting there drinking beer and rapping. We were so high and peaceful we regarded them as uninvited but potentially welcome guests. They were trying to scare us with their presence, but we made a vague gesture of invitation in the direction of the beer keg and continued with our discussion, ignoring them. This really threw them.

"But, just as easily, you could be shattered out of a subjective reverie by the sudden appearance of a uniform or even a jackrabbit. It was just a matter of mood. By this time the more respectable lush people, the straight drinkers, had started to avoid us. They were scared of getting implicated in the drug scene, and we were confined to our own clique. With them and the cops against us, we felt rejected from any normal society. The one place I still felt secure getting high was on the job."

Paul was still liked at work and was doing well. His job assignments were getting more responsible and more technically involved. Management wanted to send him to a technical college for training in chemistry and was ready to pay his way. They wanted their more promising employees to get all the technical training they could. It was a progressive firm and Paul would be able to advance rapidly. In fact, one of the senior technicians there already had nine patents in his name. It was an open and rapidly growing field—developing both improved circuitry for computers as well as more compact methods for storing electronic information. And Paul was eager to move up, but now he was getting more and more strung out on heroin.

"A lot of people are under the impression that heroin addiction completely immobilizes you, that it makes you unable to concentrate and do any kind of mentally taxing work," said Paul. "This is a fallacy. It's true after you get into that state of mind where you're so desperate you have no job and are dedicating all your time and energies to getting the next fix. But if he has a good thing going for him, a heroin addict can handle his job perfectly well. If he knows that after work he can shoot more and on weekends really let himself go. Compared to an alcoholic, for instance, who simply can't function if he's drunk, the heroin addict can be calm and efficient. The only time he can't work is when he needs a fix. When he's high, he's all right. There's another guy here at Daytop who kept a job—and this was right here in New York City—who drove a truck every day for one of the major bottling companies. He had a $150-a-day habit, which is pretty heavy, yet every day he showed at work, drove the truck, carried in the bottles, made out the invoices, and he got away with it for a long time, without anyone noticing anything wrong. That's the way I figured that things would be with me. So I was still doing my job well, but all this talk about going to college scared me. I was afraid it would interfere with the beautiful setup I had. I wanted to maintain the status quo."

Things were not proceeding so smoothly for Paul at home. His relationship with his wife was deteriorating. Because of his heroin habit, he had lost most of his interest in sex, and he suspected that his wife was seeing other men. He had never taken the marriage seriously, even less so since becoming a father. He became careless about his habit, and one night his wife discovered a hypodermic needle and a few bags of heroin hidden in his shirts. "Things came to a head fast," said Paul. "She confronted me. She asked if I was an addict. I tried to talk my way around it, but then I admitted that I was on dope. She went into a tailspin. I acted very cavalier about the whole thing, as though it were unimportant. I had a good job, I told her. I was making good money. What business was it of hers if I got high once in a while? That was my attitude, and it drove her nuts. She told me to cut it out or she'd leave me, and I didn't take that seriously. One weekend when I'd taken off and been away a few days, I came home and she was gone. And all the furniture was gone with her. I went to her job. A girl said, 'She's not here.' Then I saw her in the park with our baby and her mother. I was going to rush up to her in a fit of outrage, but a bit of reality began to settle in. I said, 'What the hell is this? What am I doing?' I got scared. Like I was to do later a lot of times, I had visions of myself at forty-five or fifty all alone with no place to go, no job, no family or friends, just all strung out on dope. It bugged me, but not for long, because I ran out to get a fix, which drowned out the feeling of reality and panic. But it was a shock that she'd actually left me. I couldn't get away from this. I was relieved that the truth had come out between us and I no longer had the burden of all that hypocrisy, but the sense of loss and failure was enormous. I didn't want to feel that either. I still had the illusion that if I pulled myself together and made the decision, I could kick all the drugs and straighten out. One thing I had going for me on that line of thought was that I'd never tried. I was sure I could. I wasn't that strung out, I thought. It was just something I didn't want to do right then. I couldn't make up my mind whether I wanted to get my wife back then or wait until I'd kicked my habit. The big decision I came to was that it would be an ideal time to take a vacation. I took two weeks off and went to live at Long Beach. The idea was that I'd take it easy, taper off drugs, evaluate my life, the different alternatives, and come to a final objective decision.

"Instead, as soon as I got to Long Beach, I ran into some old dope-fiend friends and proceeded to get completely strung out. There were no longer any controls—no job to go to in the morning, no wife to come home to at night. One of these guys had a rich brother who owned a whole chain of apartment houses, and he had a lot of money. He gave me a car to use—a 1963 Tempest—and I began peddling heroin with them to help feed my own habit. When my two weeks of vacation ran out, I called in at the job and told them I was very sick and would have to be out another week. They said okay, but when I called in the next time they said, 'Look. This thing has gone too far. We're replacing you. So either quit or be fired.' I quit, and that was the end of my electrochemical career."

Paul's friends then offered him a partnership in their operations, smuggling marijuana and heroin out of Mexico. Paul accepted. The operation turned out to be very lucrative. In his 1963 Tempest, Paul would drive down to Tijuana three times a week. Each time he would be given a telephone number and a first name before leaving. Upon arriving he placed his call. Instructions were given for the pickup, which he then made—and drove directly back across the border. For this he was paid about $1,000 a week. He usually made the trips on Tuesdays, Thursdays, and Saturdays. If there was no answer to his phone call, he would wait in town a few hours, going to Santa Rosa or a bullfight. But if he got no answer after a second attempt, Paul was supposed to go right back to California, not stay overnight. His pickup usually consisted of six ounces of heroin and thirty pounds of pot. He would keep a kilo of marijuana for himself—2.2 pounds—and sell the rest. With the heroin, it was more complicated. The stuff he bought was about 40 percent pure. Paul would cut it down four times. He would add three ounces of milk sugar to each ounce of the 40 percent heroin. That meant from the original six ounces he produced twenty-four ounces of a compound 10 percent pure. Out of each shipment Paul delivered, he kept at least an ounce of heroin for himself—in his case the ounce being cut down to between 15 and 20 percent. It would get cut at least once, possibly twice, more after he sold it, but that was none of Paul's business. He and his partners were the middlemen, the link between the Mexico wholesalers and pushers in the states. They sold the marijuana for about $100 a kilo around Los Angeles, and for $200 or $300 around San Francisco. The heroin went for $300 an ounce in Los Angeles, $600 in San Francisco. The farther north they made their sales the higher the profits were, but so were the risks. Once Paul sold a shipment of heroin as far north as Vancouver for $15,000. But, as a rule, they tried to sell each lot as soon and as close to home as possible.

"It was an ideal arrangement for a dope fiend," said Paul. "I had all the stuff and money I could use, plus the kind of sinister self-image that went with being a dealer. That was a large part of the whole routine—the self-image it provided. We only knew the guys we sold to on a first-name basis. The stuff we gave them was consistently good quality, and they trusted us. We also trusted each other. We were independent and were never threatened by any syndicate pressures.

"I averaged $1,000 a week. The car was mine outright, and my share of the rent was low. I was making no effort to get any money to my wife for her and the child's support. The money was free and clear. I might go to Palm Springs for a few days and think nothing of dumping $900. I'd fly to Las Vegas or Reno to gamble for one night. One of my favorite pastimes was to fly to San Francisco and rent a boat for $40 a day. We'd get some girls on the boat, a few ounces of heroin, a couple of cans of pot, and we were in business. I think the only time I ever felt safe during this period was on a boat. If a police launch or helicopter descends on you, you have time to hurl the stuff into the sea. Even that isn't foolproof. Heroin is often stowed in a condom, which floats. But I always felt more secure on a boat. That feeling was worth $40 a day.

"With the strong heroin I was shooting, though, I was now building up an incredible habit. When your habit gets this high, you can't kid yourself about your dependence on it, and the fear is always there of having your supply cut off. Occasionally, I wouldn't make any trips to Mexico for a few days, and I'd run out of my own supply. This would be terrible. The stuff available in California was so much weaker than what I was taking. Once I ran out of stuff when I was with a girl. She offered me some cocaine. Now, I'd had cocaine before, but only in combination with heroin—what's known as a speedball. Cocaine is an aphrodisiac. A heavy heroin habit makes you impotent, so when you want to get it up for a while, you shoot some coke along with your stuff. But this night I shot the cocaine alone. I got it up, and we had a good screw, but afterward I had the sweats and diarrhea and felt terrible. Cocaine is really a stimulant with an effect opposite to that of heroin. Instead of blocking out feelings, it makes you more aware, so when you're feeling terrible and need a fix, coke makes you feel even worse."

During this time Paul tried to be meticulous about his behavior while in Mexico. Normally, he'd fix before driving down, then once more after scoring in Tijuana, prior to driving back. Aside from that, he didn't let any pleasures or diversions interfere with his schedule. He stayed in Mexico no longer than he had to and remained as inconspicuous as possible. When he digressed from this pattern, the results were disastrous. The first time, against his better judgment, he agreed to give two addict acquaintances of his a free ride down to Mexico with him and back. The idea was just to let them have "a look around." When they got to Tijuana, Paul phoned his connection, but there was no answer. His friends told him they'd like to rest on the Santa Rosa beach for a while, so Paul left them there while he went to phone again. It was two more hours before he could make his connection and pick up the stuff. When he got back to the beach, he found that both his friends had taken overdoses, and there were poisonous yellow scorpions crawling over their bodies. Paul put his ear to their chests and found that one of the men was already dead. Death could have been caused by an overdose or by the scorpions or by a combination of both. In any case, Paul left the dead friend on the beach, and drove the other to the hospital; the friend lived but had to be hospitalized for three months. Paul managed to get away without being implicated. "It was a wierd experience," says Paul. "Very frightening. I'll never forget those yellow scorpions running all over their bodies.

It was like an omen to me of worse things that might lie ahead. But on the surface I played it cool, shrugged it off, and told myself, 'Well, you shouldn't take guys with you on trips when you score.'"

Paul admits it is only now—after going through all the changes that the emotional exposure at Daytop requires—that he sees this period of running drugs out of Mexico as being the loneliest of his life, worse than anything he'd experienced at Soledad Prison or, later, at Fort Worth. When he had had a job and a family, the drugs had at least been an escape from something real. But now there was nothing to escape from, no objective responsibilities against which he could act out the rebellious role of the addict. "When you're that strung out," according to Paul, "you project all your underlying pain and anxiety into one overriding fear—that of getting caught. It's something like these guys who can't stand the hassle of paying off a dozen different bills from month to month, so, instead, they take out one gigantic loan from the bank to cover everything, and that makes them feel better.

"Anyway, my life as a junkie was now devoid of all options. The size of my habit, rather than any flash of honesty, made me realize that I couldn't kick on my own. I'd tried cutting down, and I couldn't even do that. No. I didn't want to get arrested. I was scared of kicking and the withdrawal pains, the habit was so big. And I knew there was nothing for me in jail. I only knew that I *would* get caught sooner or later, but there didn't seem anything to do but go on with the game."

At this point Paul had been dealing out of Mexico for eight months without a hitch in the routine, except for the death of his friend on the beach, a situation from which he'd managed to extricate himself without falling under suspicion. He'd been seen as a good Samaritan, just trying to help out two fallen compatriots.

One day he got to Tijuana, phoned his connection, and was informed that the shipment hadn't arrived yet. In such a situation, he was supposed to drive right back and make no further contact until his next trip down. But this afternoon he had a problem that made him reluctant to do this. He had run out of heroin and was counting on the connection for himself. With his nerves shot and hungry for heroin, he couldn't face the prospect of driving the more than a hundred miles back home without it. After some difficulty, he managed to score on his own. It was a weak mixture though, below his customary standards, and he decided to stay the night, hoping to make his regular pickup in the morning.

He phoned his connection early, and the delivery had been made. He picked it up, fixed, and headed for the border crossing where he observed that about twenty cars were lined up ahead of him, going through some kind of inspection. "I panicked," said Paul. "I'd never crossed in the morning before, and I didn't know that this was strictly a routine inspection of Mexicans who went to work every day across the border in the States. I guess that because I'd stayed over, violating the rules of our operation, I was feeling especially vulnerable and guilty. I turned the car around and headed for Tecate, a smaller town farther east where there was another border crossing. When I went through there, I must have looked as guilty as I felt. Four immigration officers searched every inch of the car. They found the pot under the back seat and the heroin under the dashboard.

"I was taken to the San Diego County jail, but even then I tried to play it cool, saying to myself, 'Well, now at least I'll have some time to catch up on my reading.'"

Paul had three charges against him: smuggling heroin, smuggling pot, and failure to register and pay tax on the pot. The tax law was repealed by the Supreme Court in 1969 as being self-incriminating and therefore unconstitutional, but, at that time, the violation carried a sentence of up to three years. The other two charges carried sentences of from five to twenty years each. Paul's bail was set at $10,000. "So there I sat," said Paul, "while the narcotics agents tried to make incredible deals with me. They tried to impress upon me the fact that I was facing a potential of forty-three years in prison, considering that I already had a record. Of course I didn't buy that. But they did have two valid five-year charges they could intimidate me with and get me to talk. But they didn't want me to just talk. They kept saying, 'Look. We'll put everything back in the car

111

just the way it was. You drive back, make your delivery, and then we'll move in. If you cooperate with Uncle Sam, we understand there's a good chance you'll get off with six months.' It was too ridiculous a suggestion. I just wouldn't do it, aside from the question of morality, of loyalty to my partners. They wouldn't even be straight about making a deal, talking about Uncle Sam! Jesus. And setting up this elaborate trap. It was all so pointless. It wasn't as though the stuff were being delivered *up* the echelons of the drug hierarchy. It was going strictly *down* the line to the street pushers. I felt the agents were stupid, and it made me angry, so I told them to leave me alone. 'Okay,' they said. 'We'll come back in a few days, when you're kicking, and we'll see if you sing a different tune.'

"I didn't sing a different tune, but I hadn't ever kicked before. These days you hear that the symptoms of withdrawal have been exaggerated, and that it's no worse than getting over a bad case of the flu. There's some truth in this from what I've seen here at Daytop. But I had a rough time. It was the first and last time I ever kicked, and it was unbelievable, my habit had been so enormous. I vomited continuously after trying to eat, and when there was nothing to vomit, I had the dry heaves. I sneezed sometimes twelve times in a row. I had diarrhea like dysentery, and every bone in my body ached and ached and ached. The sum of it was that I didn't sleep for fourteen days, although the worst physical pain let up after a week. But I'd been prepared for something horrible, and it was no surprise. What got me was the way the federal agents kept coming back and saying, 'Are you ready to cooperate now?' That they were trying to use my withdrawal pains against me made me so angry that I wouldn't even answer them. I wanted to kill them. I refused to discuss anything with them until I'd kicked and felt better—which was two weeks after my arrest. When they realized that I wasn't going to turn anyone else in, much less cooperate in some fantastic setup, we began bargaining over my sentence. The point was that if an addict pleads not guilty, the trial can drag on forever. So they try to get you to plead guilty to one charge, and they'll agree to drop the others. In my case, I pleaded guilty to one count of smuggling heroin, and they dropped both marijuana charges. I was sentenced to five years."

There are only two federal facilities for drug addicts in this country. One is in Lexington for addicts east of the Mississippi, and the other, the western equivalent of Lexington, is in Fort Worth where Paul was sent, in handcuffs locked to a chain around his stomach, in the custody of a federal marshal. "When I got there," said Paul, "I felt good physically. I was angry and defiant and ready for the worst that the place had to offer. It wasn't until nine months later that I let any real emotions hit me, and then I broke down and cried. Prior to that, I stayed cool and angry."

Shortly after Paul's arrival, the Fort Worth authorities launched an experimental program for those addicts they judged as having the best motivation, the best chances of being rehabilitated. The program was to be administered by a psychiatrist, a psychologist, a nurse, and a social worker. Theoretically, it was supposed to be a therapeutic community, the residents having at least some control over their own lives, but, according to Paul, it was doomed from the start: "What little autonomy we had was limited to superficial privileges. There was a recreation center where we could play ping-pong and shuffleboard. There was a baseball field, a handball court, and a small library. On top of all that, there was token recognition that we were human beings, and this in itself was supposed to be a revolutionary concept."

But the basic hospital or prison dichotomy between staff and patients remained. Out of 300 addicts at Fort Worth, only 60 of them had been chosen for the special program. Those who had not been chosen for it felt discouraged and jealous; those who were developed an attitude of elitism and quickly decided to take complete advantage of their freedom and privileges. It was one of those halfway measures toward liberal reform that end by making everyone cynical and hungry for little scraps of power. Paul wanted the experimental program to work because it offered a soft life of the kind ideally suited to the withdrawn, devious ways of an addict. "Just take the daily routine," he said. "At first I worked in the kitchen. This job would occupy me from noon to one-thirty. From one-thirty to five I was free. From five to seven I would work again, and the rest of the evening was free. Some guys were clever enough to manipulate themselves into jobs that took no more than forty minutes a day. Eventually, the program became converted by us into a complete racket and con game. All it lacked was dope itself, and, on occasion, we managed to have that too."

The addicts formed a minority of the hospital's patients and were regarded with suspicion, if not downright hostility, by the staff. In an adjoining facility were some 600 mental cases, including 100 merchant marines who had caught syphilis before the discovery of penicillin. By the time the disease had been arrested by the new drug, it had already done irreparable damage to their nervous systems. These patients were at Fort Worth for life—and death. Paul was particularly bothered by the syphilis patients because they at least received some sympathetic attention from the student nurses. "On a Saturday night," said Paul, "these poor guys would have these nurses come over and socialize with them. But at the same time the staff would warn the nurses, 'Don't go near the drug addicts. They're all devious sex maniacs.' It was all right to feel sympathy for the syphilis guys. We did too. But we weren't even treated as their equals, although we were in this progressive program. I can understand not treating an addict as a human being while he's on drugs. But once we're off, can't we be taken seriously? In the same ward with the syphilis patients were schizophrenics, catatonics, and relatives of government employees, who'd gone nuts. These people were all together and got some sympathy, but the drug addicts were isolated and made to feel like social outcasts. The whole stigma of being a drug addict had never been more pronounced, despite our token privileges. The doctors, when they first came in, would try to be sympathetic. But most of them had gone into public health to stay out of the Army. They'd start with fresh attitudes, but soon they were beaten down into the same mold as everyone else. They treated it all as a nine-to-five job and tried not to get too involved. Every group there was locked in its own departmental island: the nurses, the psychologists, and the security guards. At worst we

114

were hated. At best, pitied. We lived with minimum security but in maximum isolation."

Paul thought about escaping. Under minimum security it wouldn't have been too difficult. But if he had been caught, it would have automatically added five years to his sentence, bringing the total he was facing to ten, and Paul decided not to risk it.

Under such alienating circumstances, prisoners form allegiances according to primitive links with their origins. There was a clique of whites from Nevada, of Mexicans from Albuquerque, of blacks from St. Louis. Feelings were especially bad between the whites and blacks. If a white prisoner became known as someone who befriended blacks, he'd be ostracized by his own group. That was the code of the prison. "I did the same thing," said Paul. "I rarely made friends with anyone unless he was white and came from California. There was never any peace in the ward. There were sixty of us all trying to con each other and the staff as much as possible without getting demoted to the general population. I was twenty-six at this point. I did happen to be in the clique of California guys who wanted to attain power and eventually did, but it was a struggle.

"Ward politics was really something. In the beginning, the guys who were heads of the ward were those who had the most seniority in the place and who had the most sophisticated brand of rhetoric to bulldoze the doctors with. There was a doctor there named Kraus who was trying to initiate some kind of therapy, though he didn't know what. At that time the kind of group therapy we have in Daytop, where you deal with feelings, was unheard of. To express your emotions was not encouraged. And if it had been, we wouldn't have submitted to it, from lack of trust. I think the doctors and the psychologists themselves were afraid to confront our feelings. What would happen is that this Dr. Kraus would get the most articulate of us together and ask our advice. It was so hypocritical and superficial. The only issues we discussed were whether we would get a new toaster, or a TV set, or have more free hours over the weekend. We would also discuss endlessly what form of political organization would work best in our ward. We Californians were out to get power whatever form it took—whether we had

115

to con doctors into appointing us as leaders—or whether we had to con the other residents into electing us. The number of California guys in the ward was gradually increasing, but we still didn't have enough influence to take over. I think this doctor wanted to keep us in a state of stress. He felt that if you don't keep some kind of pressure up, you don't see a change. The idea was that if we were all involved in serious power struggles, he'd be able to observe the real man emerging and come to some true conclusions about the nature of the drug addict. In other words, he pretended that he was on our side, unlike the rest of the staff, but he actually regarded us more as guinea pigs for his own cerebral experiments. It wasn't as though he ever said, 'I know what you mean. And if you do this, I'll back you.' It was more like he'd say, 'Let's try this. I'm curious to see how you'll function when it happens.' And he had the power to shoot us all back to the ranks of the general population if he wanted. In any case, he and the guys in power had some kind of agreement together, and it wasn't until he left the scene that new ward elections were held.

"By that time more California guys had entered the program, and we campaigned as the young progressives, promising to initiate reforms once we got into power. The older guys lost out. We made it sound as though they'd simply been the patsies of the doctors like Kraus. It was a triumph of rhetoric over reality, because we had no real power to make changes. The old guard was out, and we were in. That's all. The lunacy of it all is revealed in the titles we were elected to: president, vice-president, and treasurer. I was the treasurer, and my two best buddies president and vice-president. Treasurer of what? Well, I eventually became treasurer of our gambling operation.

"Anyway, the first reforms we instituted were to provide ourselves with the most comfortable rooms in the ward. One guy had a TV set. I had an FM radio, the use of which was restricted to our clique. We arranged to have pickles and cold cuts and bread smuggled up from the kitchen. I, as treasurer, benefited from the most ridiculous rule in the place. We were allowed to receive up to $50 a month to spend in the commissary in the form of ducats or coupons. It was so snobbish. Some guys

116

would get it from their parents or girl friends. Some guys wouldn't. It created a real plutocracy. One of the first reforms we instituted was to get permission to hold poker games, which became the main weekend activity of the experimental ward. Since we didn't have cash, we'd pay a guy a carton and a half of cigarettes to keep score for us. We played a dollar limit. These poker games would run from Friday night to Sunday night, and, due to the $50-a-month rule, considerable sums of money became involved. I had no allowance, but I was a good poker player, so I cleaned up. Inspired by my success at poker, I later instituted elaborate pools on the baseball, football, and basketball games, according to the season. I plowed through all the papers in the library, picked up the odds from the sporting columns, and we'd put out a daily sheet, offering odds, and accepting bets in either coupons or cigarettes. We did well."

Within this supposed therapeutic context, prestige was rated exclusively by how much one could take others for—both staff and the other residents. Or, if one could stay up all night watching television, gamble all weekend, or occasionally smuggle in some dope, one had the respect of the other inmates. These were the only functioning incentives.

Although it was done infrequently, heroin was smuggled in more easily than pills. Most often it was brought in by new prisoners entering what was called the "kick ward," and it was usually concealed in a condum in the rectum. Pot was the most difficult and unmanageable substance to smuggle in. There was considerable traffic in the herb mace. "You mix it in hot water and if you're feeling ambitious you can get a high off it equivalent to a couple of joints," said Paul. "What the hell is mace? A spice. It didn't do much for me, but I drank a lot of it when I was there because it was an emblem of power. And if we'd gotten caught drinking the stuff, we'd have been in trouble— as though it were pot or liquor.

"One of the kids in our ward had a job as a houseboy for one of the doctors. When the doctor was away, this guy broke into the medicine cabinet and brought us back Seconals, Nembutals, Benzedrine, Dexadrine, Tuinals, and Doridens. We kept what we wanted and dealt out some of the stuff to people in the main ward. It boosted our image there. Every once in a while, the doctor in charge would say, 'Is there anything wrong going on around here?' I'd say, 'No, no. Everything's fine.' I liked him, but there was no reason why I'd tell him that all these guys had pills.

"Anything contraband that entered the ward was supposed to have our approval. We wanted to exercise control over any illicit traffic. But the younger guys didn't accept our authority. Though warned against the consequences of smuggling in hypodermic needles, they wanted to try it. It was crazy because we rarely had anything to shoot in a hypodermic needle, but the idea was to have one available, in case some heroin came in. So one day a hypodermic needle was smuggled in. At the ceiling level our ward had an intricate complex of vents in several corners. These guys tried to hide their hypodermic needle by hanging it down a vent between the walls. But somebody screwed up, and, instead, the needle got dropped down into a corner of the television room, where the hacks found it. It was pretty funny, but whenever there was an incident like that, the hacks would make life miserable for us in small ways."

By this time Paul had a good job working in the laboratory. When new prisoners passed through the kick ward, they were sent to the lab for a blood test or a urinalysis; if a new prisoner had some heroin with him, he was able to transfer it there to Paul or one of the other workers. One day Paul got word that a young person coming through had some heroin with him. But the day he was scheduled to reach the lab, Paul was called into security, and told a friend of his to contact the new prisoner and make the pickup. Instead of waiting for Paul, his friend took a shot and gave himself an overdose. "His lungs collapsed and he almost died," said Paul. "There are two kinds of overdoses— this kind, when the shock of the heroin hits the system so hard that the lungs collapse. In this case, you can sometimes get the lung back in shape by holding the patient's nose, then blowing very hard into his mouth. The other kind of overdose is from sheer oversaturation in heroin. It usually happens when a guy's been shooting large amounts for an extended period of time, and eventually his system can't take any more. The first kind of overdose kills from shock, the second from just too much dope in the system. My friend was rushed to the hospital, where they performed a tracheotomy and saved his life. He didn't talk and give me or the other kid away, even though he was almost dead, and they were threatening to send him to a federal prison. In the meantime I'd gotten hold of the rest of his stuff and stashed it away in the power house. This incident got the security hacks really uptight, and one of them in particular had it in for us. We had it in for him, too, and one Saturday night this guard was sitting down, watching the movie, when we noticed that his wallet was sticking over halfway out of the rear pocket of his pants. We got ahold of the wallet. There was only a dollar in it. But we destroyed it and all the identification papers. Everyone knew what happened, but nobody talked.

"After these incidents the hacks really harassed us. They hated to have anything put over on them, and were determined to get even. It was always done in such a sneaky, malicious manner. You'd be sound asleep and suddenly they'd be yanking you out of bed, searching your sheets and your underwear. In return, we continued to try to outwit them in small ways. For instance, I managed, over a period of several months, to make two five-gallon batches of home brew—one out of raisins and the other out of sweet potatoes. Terrible stuff! But I got high whenever I could. And a lot of the pleasure came from having outwitted the hacks. Childish games, but the only satisfactions we had."

After working several hundred hours in the lab, one of Paul's duties was to assist at the autopsies performed in the prison. Whenever one of the patients suffering from syphilis died, Paul would help to remove the brain and place it in formaldehyde so that the doctors could determine the precise damage caused by the disease. Once, a seemingly healthy prisoner, only thirty-one years old, dropped dead while playing basketball. Paul helped at the autopsy where it was found that the cholesterol level of the patient's blood had been unusually high—a condition that might have been remedied if the doctors had known about it in time. "This was interesting and challenging work," said Paul. "What is even more interesting was the fact that the pathologist was a woman, about thirty-six and very attractive. Of course the worst thing to endure in all these prison programs is the total absence of any contact with the opposite sex. There wasn't much I could do about the pathologist. She was physically and professionally beyond my reach. But soon a younger woman began working in the lab as a technologist. She was twenty-five and not bad-looking, and it soon became apparent that she had eyes for me. Emotionally, she was very confused and immature. Let's face it. You'd have to be to want to get mixed up with a junkie in the Fort Worth program, but it gave me an opportunity to get some kind of a thing going. It wasn't much, really. It started with us holding hands briefly, when no one else was around, then pressing our thighs together, and then over a period of time, it got so we were necking passionately in the autopsy room. We wanted to go down, but we didn't quite have the guts—the guts or the opportunity. We couldn't lock the door of the autopsy room, and you could never tell when somebody might come barging in. It was just another diversion like going back to some tentative high school romance. The relationship went on like this for about five months, but eventually I got fed up with it. It was frustrating, and besides, I got the feeling that she enjoyed having things that way, no chance for a real commitment. I broke it off, and we parted, quietly hating each other's guts."

After Paul had been in Fort Worth for fourteen months, a pilot project was established whereby eligible inmates would be able to apply for jobs outside of the prison. Despite the bad feeling between him and the security guards—a good deal of it because of what they suspected he'd gotten away with—Paul had a good record and a total of 1,700 lab hours behind him. He applied for the outside work project and got accepted as a laboratory technician at St. Joseph's Hospital. The hours were long —from noon to midnight five days a week—but he was on his own and commuted to work and back every day on a bus. Only the chief pathologist knew that he was an inmate of the Fort Worth program. To the patients and other employees he was just another lab employee working long hours. "I liked the work and the opportunity," said Paul. "But I was on the spot. It was the first time they'd ever tried out a program like this. And it was hard because I was playing a role. No one was supposed to know that I was a drug addict. It would have been so much better if I could have been open about it, but having this job and always having to hide the truth—it was very hard. And you had to be so careful. I mean a lot of patients in hospitals are kind of crazy, and you never know when they'll do things to get you in trouble. Sex again was always a hang-up. My job was mainly hematology, taking blood counts, and urinalysis. One night I was taking a blood sample from this blond school-teacher. She was very good-looking, and she told me her arm was sore, and she asked me to rub it, and suddenly I realized that her breast had fallen against my arm and that it was inten-tional, but what could I do? I was scared. She could have reported me, if she was a nut, and no one would have listened to my side of the story.

"Oh, all very frustrating. I pretended that nothing had hap-pened, and I said as I walked out, 'Thank you for your blood.' But it was horrible, being so vulnerable in situations like that, and always having to be so careful and defensive and diplomatic. I continued to act like a gentleman wherever possible. I kept up my contacts with the guys that were dealing with mace and bringing stuff in, but I never did bring any in myself. I had a new corner room with trees outside and everything went along fine until there was this spot check. We had them from time to time for urinalysis, to see if anyone had been taking dope, and I hadn't had any heroin for months. Now this was on a Friday, just before the weekend, and they took this test and on Monday they did the spectrograph, and they told me that the specimen had come out positive. I couldn't believe it. The only thing I can figure out is one of two things. I had taken some mace and either that in some chemical manner triggered off the positive reaction or else, which is far more likely, the security hacks were out—not only after me—but after the whole work-out program, and they thought this was a way of killing two birds with one stone. I'm sure they substituted urine with heroin in it for mine. They were very angry at seeing power going from them, and guys like me working outside—it threatened their jobs in the end, if the program worked. I could never prove this, and I might be wrong, but I'm sure that's what happened, because I don't think mace can give a positive test on a heroin spectrograph. Whatever the hacks wanted to achieve, it worked. I was fired, pulled off the job. I was allowed to stay in the experimental unit, but I was put on a tractor working outdoors on landscaping all summer long, about eight or nine hours a day, cutting grass. And a chance I'd had to go to a halfway house for ninety days was killed. I worked on the landscaping crew for two months, and managed to keep my status as a leader. I was still wheeling and dealing with mace and sleeping pills and stuff like that, and I got re-elected to my job, but there was a lot of back-stabbing going on. We were getting very tough. We didn't want to lose our power and we would threaten guys if they didn't cooperate, so we got re-elected, but things were getting a little hairy. I was very disgusted because I was out driving this tractor and it wasn't my fault, and I felt that I'd been framed—and it was about this time that David Deitch with two assistants from Daytop arrived at the prison to bring some notion of the concept there. They had a film with them called *The Circle*, which showed how Daytop worked. The first reaction among all of of us was, 'Who the hell are these guys? Let's stay away from them, some kind of creeps.' Then they held a probe, which the leadership and older members had to attend, and it ran for six or seven hours. For the first time in my life I witnessed people being confronted. I got very much involved. We were asked how we felt and were told to express our emotions without there being any fear of consequences. There was one guy there who started the whole thing rolling. After finishing almost five years in the program, he'd broken out of the place and been brought back; so he had five more years in front of him. Instead of acting tough, he related to how miserable and angry he was about having screwed up and related to what was ahead of him. He dropped his cool image and began to cry until it hit all of us. Nobody before had ever cried in this program. And another guy began to talk about his father being a minister and how hurt he was when his father had been caught as a petty thief. That was one

122

reason he'd started taking drugs, to get away from the stigma of being a corrupt minister's son. Then *I* got into it, just relating to the fear and pain I'd been blocking out. I hadn't cried for a couple of years. All I knew was how to act as tough and cool as I could, and it was a very moving and touching experience just admitting to my fear and crying. David Deitch seemed to be a beautiful guy, and they all helped us kick out these emotions we'd been hiding and pushing down. Deitch told me that they wanted to start some program in the prison but that also they wanted to get people into the program which he was running now in New York, and he told me that he'd do all he could to bet me into Daytop and would I like to? 'Yes,' I said. It shook me up, this experience. It seemed like one small little different thing had happened, and it made me hopeful, where before I had just been cynical and was going to bide my time, and would probably go back to dope. I don't know, but I'd had no hope of starting something different. He told me it would take a few months and in those few months left, I was very different. We began running groups.

"We got people to listen to us about getting rugs in our room, putting couches in the living room and chairs. We started having honest groups, and people talked about what they were afraid of, which was incredible there. The one thing you would never talk about in this prison program was what you were afraid of. You might talk about how you wanted to kill somebody, but not what you were afraid of. That just would never work. Something about David Deitch and these guys from Daytop had gotten to me and I sat tight.

"After several months, on February 6, 1968, I got my mandatory release and was accepted at Daytop. I took a Greyhound bus east. It was very strange. I had been in prison over three years and eight months, and when I got to the Port Authority Terminal in New York, whoever was supposed to meet me from Daytop hadn't shown up. I went into the toilet in the men's room, and I was sitting there when two guys came into the stalls, one on either side of me and I hear them getting ready to fix. Jesus. I hear one of them take off his belt to tie around his arm, and I hear him lighting matches, and then I even see a few drops of blood hit the floor as he fixes. That was weird enough, me sitting there thinking about how nice it would be to get high once before going to Daytop, and then this guy actually leans down and *starts to hand me a bag of stuff under the partition!* Obviously, the guy had gotten confused and must have thought I was his buddy there in the adjoining stall. I cleared my throat and mumbled something out loud so they'd get the hell out of there, but the incident really shook me up.

"I called up Daytop and I said, 'What's going on? What happened?' and they said, 'You're a day early,' and I said, 'Well, tell me how to get there.' And then they gave me instructions how to get out to Daytop. It was a long trip: the subway, the Staten Island ferry, and then the bus out to Prince's Bay. I was having doubts about whether I really wanted to go there. I was scared.

"When I arrived, they put me in the prospect chair, and I had a rough interview because these guys seemed to know the number I was running. I hadn't actually had a habit for over three years, and I was using this fact to suggest that perhaps I didn't need Daytop, or at least that I was a cut above most other addicts entering the house. They wouldn't let me get away with that game. They were really angry. They said, 'You don't need us. Go on back to Texas. Go on. Get the hell out of here. We don't need guys like you around here.' It was terribly hard for me to admit that I needed help from Daytop. I could hardly say the words, much less scream them. I was still carrying with me the old jailhouse code of acting cool, strong, and arrogant. They dragged it out of me. They just kept needling away at my crazy self-image until I broke down and yelled for help. Man, was I happy when that interview was over. I'd been so scared inside and uptight for months. I broke out in a rash! They put me to work on the service crew.

"For the next few days, I had a strange reaction. I was full of anger, and an awareness of the frustration and futility of all those years was emerging. Just being in Daytop was bringing up all these suppressed emotions, and I didn't know yet how to cope with such things! To let myself freely feel emotions, but not act off them, was an ordeal for me. On the service crew, as ramrod, was this kid only seventeen, and he knew that his age and him being over me really bugged me. He never let me forget it. God, did I hate that guy, he showing me how to use a mop correctly! I felt like breaking every bone in his body. I confronted him in encounter groups. I let out all my rage. It was the first time I'd been honest about my true feelings in my life. I told this guy how I hated him, how he made me feel small and mean, that all these years of my life had been wasted and now guys like him were trying to screw me up. At least I was honest about the hatred, and the guys in the group could identify with me on that score.

"I worked like hell on my job. This anger filled me with energy, and in five weeks I was made ramrod. David Deitch called me up to his office, told me how pleased he was with my progress, and said that I could become coordinator for bringing guys to Daytop from Fort Worth in about six more months, if I kept up the good work. This had a bad effect on me. It made me feel that I had to prove myself to him. It was a goal to win approval, not something I had to do for myself. Behind this, I operated as a very cold and calculating character. I was still being the con man, saying, 'If I do this well, they'll give me that.' I wasn't really in touch with my own emotions or responding to the feelings of other people in the house. David Deitch had been in Fort Worth himself, before going to Synanon, and because of my relationship with him, and his offer to make me coordinator of the program out there, I had the feeling that people were looking at me as a kind of teacher's pet. It wasn't true, as I learned later. It was just a subjective feeling, but it isolated me. I became so out of touch that I didn't even use common sense on the job. I was more interested in exercising for its own sake what little power and authority I had. For instance, after I became department head of maintenance, we had a big music festival. In the planning stage, I was in charge of getting the stage and all the wiring set up. Then on the night of the festival, I was in charge of the traffic and parking. A certain car had been put on hold—that meant that it wasn't supposed to be driven off the grounds—because a wheel bearing was shot. But during the festival, when the night coordinator needed to make a trip, I took the car off hold on my authority.

As the night coordinator drove out the gate, the wheel collapsed, and the car ran off the road. I got smoked out for that, and I understood what had made me do it—the urge to assert my own authority, to buck the standing order. But a few days later I produced a repeat performance. The same night coordinator was in charge again, but I had temporarily relieved him, when this kid came up to me. It was Saturday night, and he asked me for permission to have a hamburger fry. Again I said, 'Sure. Go ahead,' when I hadn't the authority to say yes or no. When the night coordinator came back and learned what had happened, he really blew his stack and sent me up to the director's office for a haircut. They smoked the hell out of me, showed me how encapsulated I was, not relating to other people, and they shot me down to the kitchen detail. At the same time that I lost the job, I also lost my status as a coordinator trainee."

In fact, it wasn't just the car and hamburger incidents that resulted in Paul's being shot down again. While a coordinator trainee, he had met a girl named Betty at a Saturday-night open house, and they had been seeing each other without Paul's informing the directorship. Paul knew the rules—any kind of relationship with a girl had to be brought before the directorship. But he hated the idea of doing that and had postponed it, hoping that some side of his life could remain secret and private, outside of the controls of the house. The girl was not only attractive but was rich as well, and he felt that his chances with her might be jeopardized by too much open talk and analyzing. He wanted to have something beautiful and private outside of the Daytop codes of loving concern and responsibility. His idea was to tell them something, so his conscience would be clear, but not enough so that the directorship would have the right to interfere.

All of this came out in Paul's haircut. The directorship decided Betty would have to visit Daytop as his girl, and they would have to see how she could handle it in the long run. In the short run, it worked out very well. Although she had been spoiled and pampered, and her parents had a great deal of money and social connections, she committed herself to Daytop, assisted in various jobs, and was accepted.

"Anyway, after being shot down, I felt very bad," said Paul. "I thought nobody trusted me because of my devious ways. I got desperate. Also, Betty and I had not gone to bed together yet, which bothered me. We asked for permission. The directorship said we weren't ready for that yet. 'The relationship has to mature more,' they said. A few weeks later the sex permission was finally given. We went to Central Park. We were both very nervous. We went back to her apartment, and it took us a while to unwind. I was so starved for sex after all that time in Daytop and prison. We made love several times, and I was sweating and breathing so hard I ended up getting a terrible cold.

"So the sex was great, but we had problems. Betty's parents didn't want her going around with an ex-addict. She told them it was none of their business, yet I wondered sometimes if her feeling for me wasn't just a means of her asserting her independence from her parents.

"It was during this time that the big split was developing at Daytop. Although I felt a strong allegiance to David Deitch for having brought me to Daytop, I saw a lot wrong in the house; the opposition to David had a strong case. In the end, though, I was too unsure of myself to make a decision or commitment to join either side. Instead, I left with Betty and went to live with her out on Long Island. This was a spooky experience. I began to feel more and more like the poor drug addict who'd fallen in love with the rich debutante. That seemed to be where it was at. Then the weirdest things happened. Her older brother came to see us. He took me aside and said, 'You'll end up causing our mother to have a stroke. We just can't afford to have a drug addict in the family.' Then he literally offered me money to leave her. The complete arrogance with which he openly offered the bribe made me feel so humiliated, that I was tempted to shoot dope behind it, but I didn't.

"I went to talk to Betty's psychiatrist, and he was sympathetic, eager to help us work things out together. He was on the board of an outfit called GROW, which was a kind of community project bringing ministers, social workers, parents, and other interested groups together to deal with drug addiction. Technically, I'd been free of drugs for a long time now, and he encouraged me to take a job in GROW running groups as an ex-addict. But when this kind of challenge was presented, I realized in my gut that I wasn't ready to run groups like that, that I still had a long way to go. I'd heard that Daytop was reorganizing again under Ronnie Brancato and Charlie Devlin. I called Charlie, and he said they wanted me back in the house, but that I'd have to make up my mind within four days. I went to see them—Dr. Casriel was there too—and I talked about how I was scared to go back, that I'd be looked on as a coward for not having joined either side. They pointed out that this was my central emotional problem, being unable to commit myself completely, being afraid to assert my strongest qualities, to simply be myself. They said I was really needed in Daytop, but that my self-doubts were keeping me from believing this. I went back to the house the next day.

"There was hostility and suspicion from certain people in the house who looked at me as a splittee and resented the fact that I had a kind of amnesty and was allowed to keep my resident status. But I confronted these hostilities in groups and began to open up in other ways. I had a good marathon in which Marilyn and Wilbur John, an older, black resident, helped me to get down to the real painful feelings I'd been blocking out for so long. I went back to the pain of needing the father love I'd never had. I saw how, to insulate myself from the anger and hurt he'd caused me, I tended to blame his desertion of us all on my mother. And there was more to it. I saw that because he was a phony and a weakling that I'd been afraid I was too. And that this had made me suspicious of those qualities he'd always preached to me—courage, stamina, and independence. The group made me see that these qualities were all in me, but that this old pain had been holding me back, making me reserved, controlled, and cautious. I cried and reached out and asserted for the first time how much I needed to be loved.

"The house at Swan Lake was being opened up, and I was made coordinator of operations up there. It worked out well, and I earned a lot of respect. When I came back to Staten Island six weeks later, plans were being made to completely renovate the Fourteenth Street house and restore it. Though it had been open before, we'd only been using a fraction of it, and most of the some 200 rooms there had never even been cleaned out. I was now made coordinator of that operation. I started working with twelve guys; this number was increased to thirty when we realized how big the job was.

"The Fourteenth Street house is a six-story mansion. Previously a convent, it looks in some ways more like an eighteenth-century brothel with ceilings seventy-five feet high, sixteen-foot brocaded mirrors, enormous columns. Just fixing up the ground floor, we used 2,000 yards of carpeting, 250 gallons of paint, 100 pounds of plaster, 300 pounds of spackle. We worked there for seventy-nine days, and I worked about sixteen hours a day. At the same time we were pulling new people into Daytop, running about ten prospect interviews a day. It was a magnificent job. The house was beautiful.

"When we'd finished, Betty and I went to St. Thomas for a week's vacation. When we got back, I was made senior coordinator at Fourteenth Street, and Betty had a paying job, working in the business office. There was still a lot of strain between us, and it didn't help that I'd never told her that I'd been married and had a child and that my wife had divorced me while I was in Soledad Prison. That was still the old dope fiend in me, holding back the truth and compromising in order to keep things comfortable, to avoid friction. When this came out, I was dragged into the director's office, and he said, 'Are you getting into that bag again! We won't let you operate that way here. That's all.' I felt really bad about it, but Betty and I went into a couple's group, and we had the whole thing out. It seemed, though, as I got stronger, Betty became more anxious and unsure of our relationship. It wasn't long before she began dropping hints to the tune that she wanted to go on seeing me, but that it would be good for her if she began dating some other guys occasionally. 'Would I mind?' she wanted to know. I just couldn't see it, and I knew I was right. I was beginning to feel I really had something to offer a girl beyond good sex, and I couldn't accept her seeing other guys for sociability but keeping me in reserve for weekends. And that's where it was at, I felt pretty certain. I told her that, if that's how she felt, we would have to stop seeing each other altogether.

"We did. That was my first crack at going with a girl whose world I'd never been a part of and having it all end just the way I might have imagined—my not fitting in quite all the way—and her getting restless and unhappy and wanting to hang out more with people of her own background. It was like we'd both learned something, but it was all over, and I hated that. Shortly after I broke up with her, I became senior coordinator at Staten Island, then again at Fourteenth Street. That's the roughest job I ever had. You're right in the middle, between the directorship and the residents. The pressure's enormous, but I'm beginning to think that I thrive on pressure. It's bad enough in the house, but one of the most difficult things that happened to me was going with the drama group to put on *The Concept* in the Netherlands. I went ahead to clear the way. The problems I ran into were unbelievable. We were scheduled to put the play on in an enormous beer and coffee house in Amsterdam called the Paradisio. I went there and found that it was a place where everybody was drunk and smoking pot, and I had to take a firm stand and declare that we couldn't put the play on in an atmosphere like that. There's a very strong movement going in the Netherlands to legalize pot. There's hardly any heroin problem there, so neither the young people nor the government officials, both for and against pot, are quite able to understand the horror of the drug problems in this country. In Amsterdam I found a place that Alcoholics Anonymous let us use to present the play in. It went over beautifully, there was a crowd of 700 that gave us standing ovations. But in Rotterdam these terrible questions would get asked, which the cast wasn't quite able to field: 'Why do you prostitute yourselves this way, putting on this kind of a play? What are you, reactionaries—against the legalization of pot?' I had to get out there on the stage and try to explain where things were at; these kids in the play were from America where heroin is being sold now in the grammar school playgrounds. And the kids were confused in a foreign country. All this beautiful food was around, but they missed hamburgers and Cokes and hot dogs, and they were scared, and it made me realize for myself how scared we dope fiends are of any situation in which we might not be accepted, in which we might be misunderstood and people would turn against us. For my own part, I had to go through experiences I never thought I'd be capable of handling. I appeared on television with the mayor of Rotterdam. I went to a party and met the American ambassador. It was like for twenty-five days I myself was an ambassador from America, having to keep my cool, and through all this we had terrible technical problems. One of the girls in the play fell down coming off the stage and splintered her hip and had to go to the hospital, so that we were short one player for the performance in Rotterdam. I've never been under such strain in my life, and I began drinking too much. But overall, the trip was a fantastic success, and the strangest thing is this: that after pulling all this off, when I got back to New York, I was even more terrified than ever of socializing outside of Daytop, of just going to a party where there were people I didn't know, and of being accepted. Sure, I was a strong man in Daytop, but still there was always that fear that I couldn't fit in anywhere else. This is the hardest thing for me still. That fear of not being accepted when you're on your own.

"I'll be up for graduation soon. After that they've let me know that I'll be in line to become an assistant director. Once I've graduated I'm going out to California on a week's vacation to see my family. My mother and I have been writing to each other. My kid brother is twenty-two and just back from Vietnam. My sister's eighteen and about to graduate from high school. I don't even know them. I only remember having to baby-sit for them while my mother was out working, and how I hated it! It was so long ago, when my mother threw me out of the house, and they all gave me up as a loser, like my father. He's probably still out there, bewildered and scared and guilty, feeling like a failure, if he isn't dead already. Let's face it. I'll probably never see him again, just as I'll never see my own son, either. My ex-wife's remarried, and they've just sent me adoption papers to be signed. I'll sign them. It's best that way. But I wish there was some way of letting my father know where I'm at these days."

Epilogue: The Concept

SINCE 1965 I have been observing the results of treating drug addicts with techniques that originated in Synanon through Chuck Dederich, a nonprofessional, who was not limited by the framework of orthodox psychiatric thinking. Because we as professionals did not have a practical theoretical technique of effective treatment, it is no wonder that relatively few of us ventured into this area as therapists. Paradoxically, we sometimes understand the nature of the illness, of the maladaption, only after rehabilitation has been established, occasionally by accident rather than design. The same is true in many cases of pure and applied science: treatment is sometimes stumbled upon before the etiology has been fully uncovered.

Since I was most familiar with Adaptational Psychodynamic theory, it was to this theory I looked to find an explanation for the success of the new treatment technique. To recapitulate part of the adaptational theory which immediately concerns us: adaptational as well as Freudian psychodynamics states that the basic motivational forces of human behavior are purposeful and goal-directed. In general, behavior is designed to avoid pain and gain pleasure. The adaptive responses in situations of

133

danger (which is an anticipation of pain) is either flight and/or fight. Flight is integrated through a perception of danger, the emotion of fear, and escape from the source of danger; fight is integrated through a perception of danger, the emotion of rage, and the intent to destroy the source of danger. This theory is fine as far as it goes. But it fails to show that there is a *third* major defense mechanism used to cope with the anticipation of danger or pain. This mechanism is neither fight nor flight. It uses neither the emotions of fear nor rage and may be called detachment, using the nonpainful "emotion" of withdrawal. Just as a turtle puts his head into a shell, so do some people withdraw from the pain of awareness, the pain of reality. It is now theorized that *those people whose primary mechanism of defense is detachment are those who fit into the psychiatric classification of character disorder.*

By successfully removing themselves from the pain of reacting to stress, they have spent their energy reinforcing, by encapsulation, their isolation into a nonpainful state of functioning. Like its sister defense mechanisms of fight and flight, the psychodynamic defense of detachment may have been a very realistic one in the individual's early experience. Once patterned and ingrained, however, detachment very frequently becomes an intrapsychic fortress of one's own making. The patient has taken flight without fear into a fortress in which he feels secure, but in which, realistically, he is quite isolated, incapacitated, and imprisoned. His original fortress has become his stockade. The longer the individual stays in his own jail, the thicker the walls become through secondary encapsulation, with the result that the individual becomes less and less able to cope with the problems of everyday living.

Once this intrapsychic world with relatively little tension is evolved, the individual will overtly or covertly fight anyone who attempts to remove him from his prison-fortress, from his encapsulated shell of detachment. Once the adaptational mechanism of withdrawal and detachment is solidified and operates as a primary mechanism, the standard psychoanalytic techniques using introspection and observation are useless. The individual patient, though he hears, cannot be reached. Though he knows, he will not change. He will avoid the truth with or without outright lies. Though he may pay lip service to treatment, he spends conscious and/or unconscious psychic energy in reinforcing his defensive detachment by a secondary encapsulation. Usually pleasurable, the encapsulative shell can be made out of alcohol, drugs, narcotics, homosexuality, delinquency, or just a quiet emotional detachment from all meaningful emotional relationships without necessarily being asocial or antisocial. As a matter of fact, encapsulation could be socially productive—the shell can be reading in the library every spare minute, being up in the attic with a stamp collection, down in the cellar with the tool chest, or even in the office with patients. The detached person tends to identify with people who have similar shells. This gives him pleasurable reassurance and reinforcement.

If we forcefully remove one means of encapsulation—one shell —such as heroin, the individual will seek a substitute encapsulation such as barbiturates or alcohol.

A distinction should be made at this point between a neurosis and a character disorder. Feelings such as fear, anger, guilt, and depression are painful to experience and therefore motivate the affected person to ameliorate the pain. These feelings may become so painful that they will prevent the neurotic person from functioning; but even if rendered helpless, the person remains in tremendous pain. This is the situation of the neurotic. Like a person with a toothache, he seeks professional help to alleviate his suffering. He will do anything and everything the professional commands to alleviate the pain. The person with a character disorder, however, may feel no pain. Although his teeth or personality are in a state of decay, and although he runs the risk of losing all his teeth, or all his functioning, he does not race to the professional, be it doctor or dentist, and frequently, when forced to go for an appointment others have made for him, he fails to keep it. He knows his teeth are bad, and he also knows he should go to the dentist, but he fears the dentist will hurt and he knows his teeth don't hurt at the moment. He uses all kinds of rationalizations and excuses for not going to the dentist and says, "Perhaps I'll go tomorrow." Of course tomorrow never comes. He occasionally develops an acute toothache and comes running, screaming at the dentist to do something about the pain. But once the pain is alleviated, he fails to keep the next appointment to do something for his rotten teeth. If a little pain remains, he will take pills or alcohol in preference to returning to the dentist.

Like people with rotten teeth, those with character disorders, especially drug addicts, have little if any internal motivation to seek help. This is what we, as professionals, have been up against in the treatment of the character disorder, and the problem is how these patients can be treated efficiently through a psychotherapeutic process. The more completely the mechanisms of primary detachment and secondary encapsulation are employed, the more immature and defective is the emotional level and the personality development. A human personality, like a flower, cannot grow in a closed box. When an individual utilizes withdrawal early in life or, even in later life, uses emotional detachment as a total defense mechanism, his character stops growing, regresses, and atrophies.

The problem in treatment becomes obvious. One must first remove the encapsulating shell, and thereafter prevent the individual from withdrawing into detachment by acquiring any other kind of encapsulating shell. Then, once exposed to the light of reality, powerless to isolate himself without his fortress-prison-stockade of encapsulation, he is in a position to be taught how to grow up. For the primary addict—those to whom drug addiction is a complete way of life—a full-time institutional therapeutic environment must be utilized to enable the individual to grow up and develop emotionally, socially, culturally, ethically, morally, sexually, and vocationally. This is no small undertaking, but nothing less will suffice. These principles underline our efforts and our treatment techniques at Daytop.

Empirical observation and research at Daytop has shown that there are only two simple proscriptions needed for adequate treatment: (1) no physical violence; (2) no narcotics or other chemicals, and, by inference, no other shells under which to hide. By these two simple prohibitions we have successfully eliminated fight and withdrawal, two of the three ways an individual copes with pain or danger. There is only one avenue left open to him, only one reaction, only one mechanism of defense which he can utilize, and that is by reacting to real and imagined stresses and strains, real and imagined pains and dangers—by fear.

Motivated by fear, the addict can do one of two things. He can stay at Daytop and attempt to cope with his fears, or he can run out the door, sometimes never to return, frequently to return again at some later date. From the records of our six years of experience, we now anticipate that 50 percent of those who come to Daytop will sooner or later remain. We do not know what happens to the other 50 percent who will never return. Perhaps they are dead. Perhaps they are in jails, in hospitals, perhaps they are still attempting to be drug addicts. Perhaps they have stopped taking drugs themselves. Perhaps they are on methadone or in some other treatment facility.

Why does the addict voluntarily stay at Daytop? The answer is the genuine love and responsible concern shown to the entering members by the residents. Even though the identification in Freudian terms is that of a narcissistic object type, the addicts stay long enough to develop healthier bonds such as anaclitic identification and, finally, a positive transference to the Daytop community.

How does identification at Daytop evolve? First, the addict usually comes in as a last resort, his motivations apparently identical to those seen in the addict applying for admission to any voluntary institution. There is no place else to go. Frequently, he only wants to stay until the "heat's off" on the outside, or because he is so physically ill and desperate that he needs a haven to rest and rehabilitate. None, early in the Daytop movement, and very few even now, come in with the hope or expectation of really being cured.

The addict sees the members of Daytop, a few of whom he might have known or heard of on the street, who seem happy and functioning. At first he feels certain that they must be getting their drugs surreptitiously or that they are "conning" him for reasons not yet apparent. But the addict is too tired and sick to think about the reasons. He knows that the first thing he has to do is to free himself of the physiological need. He is dismayed when he learns he has to do this without the aid of any drugs. As he stays at Daytop, he is surprised that he goes through "cold turkey" relatively free of pain in contrast to the unbearable pains he experienced while he was kicking his habit in jails, hospitals, or on the street. People about him are busy talking, eating, lecturing, working, ironing, listening to music. He finds himself being drawn into conversation or being a fourth for cards. If the pains get too severe, someone offers to massage his muscles. It becomes a matter of personal pride to ignore the pains as much as possible. He is aware that everyone around him has gone through the same thing, and he doesn't want to be considered weak.

This is just the opposite of what happens outside of Daytop where the more he complains, the more sympathy he hopes to obtain, and the higher his status for having been a "junkie" with a large habit.

After a few days, the addict feels a little chagrined and very surprised at having kicked with comparatively little pain, discomfort, or exhibitionism. He feels the others have tricked him into diminishing his addiction and his pains. He feels rather helpless, because behavior patterns he used on the street in reference to kicking the habit had no chance of being utilized here. He feels unmasked in front of "ex-hypes" who seem to know his every thought, mood, and feeling. They good-naturedly ridicule and laugh at any attempt he makes at "conning" the group into pitying or babying him. But they are not hostile to him, nor is he rejected by them. *It is as if he cannot communicate with the members of Daytop using his patterns of thinking, feeling, and behavior from the street. Only if he listens to them and does what he is told does he feel he is in communication.*

He starts to plan to leave as soon as he's strong enough. He is surprised to find the group can read his mind—they good-naturedly laugh at him as one would who sees an infant struggling to walk. They tell him, "Wait till the three-month depression sets in." They play on his curiosity and challenge his manhood to stick it out. By this time, the new member begins to realize that the older members actually are off "junk" and actually are as happy and well as they say.

A new awareness emerges. At this time the addict begins to wonder what Daytop is all about. He asks questions. He starts to cooperate. He goes to work. He does what he is told to do. He accepts the truth of the statement, "The only thing a junkie knows when he gets here is how to shoot dope." He accepts the criticism in his everyday relationships—the "pull-ups"—and the exaggerated ridicule and hostilities both in the regular encounter groups and in the special sessions known as "haircuts" in which several of the older residents confront an individual on his failings in the house, giving him firm suggestions for future behavior. When a cardinal rule of the house has been broken or another resident of the house has failed to report it, a GM or general meeting is called, which is like a "haircut" given by the total membership.

The new member also learns to think and communicate verbally in planned seminars and to talk out during organized public-speaking periods. He finds, and is surprised to see, that his behavior is changing. He gleefully "Daytops" the newer members. He is constantly reminded of his own sickness by seeing the newest members in their days of illness.

He becomes involved in a job-status system at Daytop. He attempts to get off the dishpan and toilet details. His pathologically aggressive or manipulative attempts to prove himself are picked up immediately by the group. Again he is embarrassed, ridiculed, scolded, laughed at. With his new association and his new environment, his "code of the street" values change. It is now a matter of honor to "squeal" on one's self and others. The Daytop law of being honest with yourself and others takes hold. No secret, however personal, has any immunity. There is no pleading the Fifth Amendment. One's past and present behavior and thoughts are now opened up to everyone's inspection.

At this point, after three to six months in Daytop, the second critical time of awareness is reached. The ninety-day "hump," as they call it, is the hour of departure for some because they cannot take the pain of emerging emotional self-awareness. At last they are beginning to become aware that their manipulative behavior really cannot work. They begin to realize just how irresponsible they are, what a mess they have made of their lives. As the repressed and unconscious feelings become conscious, the pain of depression, the panic of fear, and the dread of strong guilt develops. Some awaken with frequent repetitive nightmares, just as people who were in concentration camps develop nightmares *after* they are freed from their imprisonment. Those who do leave Daytop at this stage are usually pleading to return within a week or two. On leaving, they may again take the narcotic way into a world of insensitivity to pain, but to their great surprise *and panic,* they find drugs are no longer effective in the same way. They have become too aware of the real world now to be lulled into a false sense of security by heroin. It is only through constant understanding and support that members are able to weather the emotional storms of this troubled period. Eventually, though, the addicts find they are living through emotional pain they once thought impossible to bear without drugs. And they live through it without the aid of drugs, alcohol, sleeping pills, or even tranquilizers.

This brings the addict to a third level of awareness, when he can say to himself, "I *am* able to live in the stream of life without pills or narcotics." This new awareness, plus the assurance from the senior members that "this depression won't last," and the constructive work in which he is now engaged, gradually brings the addict out of his depression.

Entering now onto a fourth level of awareness, the addict re-evaluates everything that has gone on before. He is now a "missionary" in search of "gut-level" truth. This is a term used in Daytop to describe the purely emotional, resonant, honest feelings that are comparable to those of people in analysis who have finally felt their visceral affective emotions. The addict is no longer so afraid to face himself. This stage lasts for about another year. During this time he is emotionally maturing. He has found a purpose and a positive direction in life. He reports those subjective feelings and attitudes which he realizes are immature. He "cops-out" spontaneously in the encounter groups. He attempts to become objectively critical of his own performance. He is surprised to be offered better jobs at Daytop, jobs that he may now feel unworthy to accept but which, six months before, he felt were beneath him. This feeling of unworthiness and inadequacy is attacked by others in and out of groups as being neurotic. By the end of eighteen to twenty-four months a new personailty has emerged—one strikingly different from that of the addict who entered.

During this process, the member is given two prescriptions, which the residents at Daytop call: (1) going through the motions and doing the thing, and (2) acting as if. By "going through the motions and doing the thing," they mean that you must do as you are told whether you like it or not, whether you understand it or not, whether you think it's fair or not, sensible or not, rational or not. As a matter of fact, Daytop doesn't care what the individual thinks or feels about it. They insist that the member do what he is told to do, and by so doing, go through the motions. When an individual complains that he doesn't know exactly how to do what he is told, he is then given prescription number two—"act as if":

> Act as if you knew what to do.
> Act as if you had the experience.
> Act as if you are mature.
> Act as if it's going to be successful.
> Act as if you are going to grow up and get well.
> Act as if you are already well and adult.

When people go through the motions of acting as if, they start thinking as if, and finally feeling as if. The time lag between acting as if one can get well, for instance, and feeling as if one could get well, takes from three to six months.

Treatment can also be understood and used as a communication and educational technique. An entering member is taught first to identify, understand, verbalize, and express his feelings in a comprehensible fashion. He is made aware that those undifferentiated somatic painful feelings that he has experienced on a visceral and emotional level, those feelings that he has never allowed to emerge on a conscious intellectual level, are nothing more than fear, anger, guilt, pain, and depression. He sees that these are emotions experienced by all humanity and not exclusive to what he felt was the mystical, para-human called the drug addict. He no longer sees his plight as being unique. As his defensive tools, crutches, and weapons are removed, he becomes aware that there is no difference between himself and others like him, and that there is no difference between others like him and the rest of humanity.

Central to the Daytop therapeutic process is the concept of equality—peer relationship. Historically, the treatment of emotional and behavior disorders has always been the province of authority figures. We have called these authority figures witch doctors, priests, holy men, faith healers, doctors, alienists, and psychiatrists. Society in general and the individual in particular have delegated to these men not only the rational authority due them, but also an irrational authority premised upon the possession by them of magical omnipotence in one form or another. Two hundred years ago the mainstream of Western society ceased ascribing magical curative powers to its doctors and priests. But the sick or incapacitated individual, in his state of helplessness, frequently or unconsciously attributes magical power to his psychiatrist or other healer. Modern psychiatry, stemming from the basic concept of Freudian theory, attempted via psychoanalysis, to use rational authority to re-educate the irrational authority the patient delegates to the doctor. Unfortunately, psychoanalysis is not only a very long and costly process, but is effective only with those personality structures that are both basically adult (vs. childlike) and neurotic (vs. character-disordered) to begin with. All the other categories, as shown by the table below, are to a greater or lesser extent unable to utilize psychoanalysis.

The peer group process, as practiced in Daytop, is so constituted that it does not allow the patient to delegate magic powers to the therapist(s) and prevents anyone, out of concern, from assuming responsibilities that, in reality, he cannot fulfill. The entering member is treated as an equal, a peer, by both the group and therapist or group leader. It is assumed by all the members of the group that the new member's potential for healthy functioning is basically equal to any other in the group, including the group leader, who makes no secret of his once being in the

BASIC PERSONALITY TYPES

Level of Personality Integration	Psychotic	Neurotic	Character Disorder
Adult	Psychotherapy with psycho-pharmacology	Reconstructive analytic therapy	Classical forms of treatment relatively ineffective
Adolescent	"	Perhaps reconstructive therapy	"
Childlike	"	Reparative therapy	"
Infantile	"	Supportive therapy	"

new member's spot. The entering member is quickly told that there is no magic, only hard work. We can teach, but the member must learn; no one can do the work for him or learn the lesson of feeling, thinking, and behaving for him. Each must learn for himself. Each learns that the more he attempts to involve himself in teaching his peers, the more he learns for himself. In other words, if Criminal A attempts to rehabilitate Criminal B, Criminal B may not be rehabilitated by A's activity, but A will almost certainly benefit.

The new member soon learns that others around him have no magic gifts. Some have inherent special attributes that make them better in some areas than in others, but all have the potential for happiness. He learns that he can be as mature, secure, adequate, lovable, and effective as all those around him.

Not only is there no "we-they" situation such as we the patients, they the therapists, or we the prisoners, they the prison authorities, but neither is a false therapeutic contract able to be established. The nonverbal, unconscious transfer of magical curative powers cannot be consummated. The patient-member soon learns that he is not only responsible for, but capable of, his own growth and development. The whole concept of who is responsible for "getting well" or growing up is clearly defined.

Although this principle of peer relationship and self-responsibility pervades every area of activity at Daytop, it is perhaps most dramatically illustrated in the central tool of communication and education in Daytop known as the encounter group. Instead of the polite and inconsequential type of group therapy procedure the new member may have experienced at clinics or in prison, where the rule "don't pull the covers off me and I won't pull them off you" prevails, the group therapy process at Daytop is based on authentic human encounters of the here and now. The group concentrates on the daily behavior of the group member rather than becoming bogged down in speculation about possible early childhood trauma which may explain "why" a resident became an addict. The group sessions are aimed at providing a "gut" experience, free from any phony attempts at self-defense, self-deception, or self-pity. Honesty, even of the most painful kind, and integrity are the marks of group therapy sessions at Daytop. They constitute a unique form of group interaction for the creation of aggressive and provocative interchange. The groups consist of seven or eight members, and usually meet three times a week for two hours. Frequently, the strains and petty disputes of the day, which might otherwise flourish into disabling tensions, are explored and exploded at these sessions. Members are urged to spew out their hostilities and negative feelings instead of keeping them bottled up inside.

In the peer group encounter residents are offered an opportunity to meet with any other member of the house to confront him over some grievance, by merely leaving the name, along with his own, in a box reserved for that purpose. This is known as "dropping a slip" on someone. Also, the composition of the sessions changes from meeting to meeting, so that before long, each member will have had an encounter with most other members. The membership of the groups is balanced as to sex, resident status, verbosity, and aggressiveness of members. It should be noted that, although encounter groups are frequently spiced with profanity and gutter dialogue, such language is not tolerated at any other time than during these two-hour sessions. In fact, the use of profanity outside an encounter may cause disciplinary action or provide grist for the next encounter mill.

The peer encounter is the most democratic of institutions, with all members having equal rights, and permission granted everyone to question, attack, or probe anyone else. No restrictions are placed on the use of exaggeration, sarcasm, or ridicule. The aim is constructive confrontation—the lack of which is endemic throughout our society. Most people fear the consequences of challenging and being challenged. If a child disagrees with his parents, he is scolded, punished, or rejected. If he disagrees with his teachers, he is reprimanded, expelled, or failed. If he disagrees with his boss, he may be fired for insubordination, recalcitrance, or personal incompatibility. If one disagrees with the social power structure, he may be considered a traitor, criminal, rabblerouser, coward, anarchist, and fascist. Disagreement with any authority within our culture gives one a stamp of social disapproval. Translated into a peer relationship, the attitude becomes, "I'll mind my own business. If I try to help, I'll only get hurt. If I reach out and show my concern by expressing constructive criticism, I leave myself open and vulnerable to *their* criticism." Yet constructive challenge and mutual involvement between equals are precisely what is needed for emotional growth to take place in the therapeutic community.

In addition to the two-hour encounter groups, extended sessions, known as probes, are held periodically. In a probe, which lasts up to twelve hours, one particular problem, such as prejudice or homosexual fear or guilt, is emotionally discussed and intensively explored. Finally, even more extended groups known as marathons, which last from thirty to fifty hours, are held every few months. In a marathon, the emphasis is on getting each participant to get directly in touch with basic emotions of fear, pain, anger, and love, which have been withdrawn, controlled, and hence "turned off" during his addiction, and, usually, long before that. An attempt is made to work through the four basic emotional problems that almost everyone has: (1) the inability to accept love; (2) the inability to express anger; (3) the inability to give love; and (4) the inability to accept anger. Once a person is able to feel and express all his emotions, he is able to realize that he is lovable, and entitled to be loved, without the

145

expectation of pain or danger. He becomes aware of his own identity. He starts to see himself as a real person.

In addition to work in groups, a sustained effort is made to transmit some concept of the stimulation that is possible from the cultural endeavors of the larger society, which most drug addicts have managed to elude during their lifetimes. To this end, seminars are held each day from one to two P.M., during which time some abstract, philosophical subject is discussed.

At the beginning, the new resident finds this experience puzzling and confusing. Why talk about some obscure paragraph in a work by Schiller? Why get excited about the composition of the solar system? Isn't he having enough problems just getting himself straightened out? But gradually, he feels encouraged to make some comment of his own, and, before long, he becomes an active participant in these meetings. They help him learn to communicate. He has to get up on his own two feet for a few minutes and speak on a given topic. He must take a position, voice an opinion, speak up on what he believes. It becomes a tool of the environment, designed to help him overcome the fear of expressing himself, of speaking to others. It is a sort of mental drill, an exercise in the use of words, as physical drill exercises the muscles. In this way, he is enabled to overcome the embarrassment and diffidence he feels in public, while broadening the scope of his thoughts and ideas. Perhaps once a week the seminars are used to prepare individuals for speaking engagements outside of Daytop at schools and community groups. Mock public speaking is followed by very specific constructive criticism.

All the daily housekeeping tasks at Daytop are performed by the residents themselves. They are grouped into departments—expediters, maintenance, kitchen, commissary, service crew, and procurement teams—each with its own coordinator, department head, ramrod (foreman), and workers. The coordinators, who are house members of the highest proven abilities, are responsible to a senior coordinator, who is responsible to the assistant directors, who, in turn, are responsible to a resident director (one for each house). Above him is the deputy director and overall program director, who is responsible to the medical psychiatric superintendent and to the Daytop board of directors.

146

The housekeeping tasks are assigned by the house director, or his assistants, on the basis of discussions with supervisory personnel. The lower-status chores are assigned to newcomers, or as a form of sanction or "learning experience" for older residents who have infringed upon some of the house rules.

It has been noted time and again that workers in prison labor systems are encouraged to be nonproductive, dilatory, and contentious. Prison-developed attitudes, which affect almost all addicts to some degree, prejudice their abilities to adjust subsequently in the labor market. At Daytop, on the other hand, the prevailing values are those of the so-called Protestant Ethic: hard work, family responsibility, regard for others, thrift, and concern for the future. Approval of, and attachment to, these virtues come in time to replace those of the addict reference group exclusively concerned with "connections" and getting the next "fix"; boasting about being a "boss addict"; attempts to turn the values of the "square" world upside down; "hustling" and prostitution; avoidance of family and community responsibility. All these become negative values at Daytop Village because of the socializing pressures of the community and the example of senior residents who serve as "role models."

The positive exploitation of the normal individual's striving for status is an important Daytop tool. Residents are reminded that nobody gets "something for nothing." The member who "does his thing" is rewarded by recognition and promotion up the status ladder; if he does well enough for long enough, there is no position he cannot attain. The social system of Daytop is organized in a way that can be used as a means of effecting behavioral change by exploitation of the desire to improve one's status. Other tools for reinforcing a resident's sense of responsibility and social morality include the issuance of privileges such as letters and visits from relatives, telephone calls, and walks to the neighborhood community.

The process of reforming a human personality has never been easy, and when the subject is a drug addict whose adherence to the values of a highly deviant subculture is well known, any undue optimism about a quick cure would be misplaced. Nevertheless, under the pressures of change exerted at Daytop, resi-

147

dents are in a position to go into "re-entry" after about twelve months. This means that residents re-enter the community via one of Daytop's three SPAN operations—teaching, educating, and inducting using addicts into rehabilitation. SPAN, which stands for Special Project Against Narcotics, consists of three storefront facilities—two on Manhattan's Lower East Side and one in Westchester County. SPAN serves five functions:

(1) Residents in the re-entry stage have to confront the neighborhood pressures and attitudes that gave rise originally to their own use of drugs. It helps to test the recovering resident's capacity to withstand the pressures and temptations of outside society.

(2) It enables the local community to be aware of Daytop so that hard-core addicts in the area can get off the streets and into a Daytop facility. It serves as the initial intake process for new prospects, where they are interviewed and eventually referred to one of the three houses.

(3) It exists as a counter-epidemic in an area where the use of drugs is high. It confronts the early and peripheral drug users with an alternative, and tries to reorient them right at the storefront through group lectures, seminars, and interaction with the Daytop staff. It offers the local community a helping hand, but its constant motto is to help a person do for himself, rather than do for a person.

(4) It works on community attitudes, explaining how these can contribute to the problem of addiction. It develops groups of community people, unifying them, training leaders, and then makes them self-sufficient in dealing with community problems. In other words, it develops a force of agents for social change.

(5) It works together with professional agencies, sharing knowledge and information which would help them in dealing with addicts; it works closely with the Daytop Parents' Association.

The resident works in re-entry for about two months. He is now ready for stage two, which means living in and working out. In second stage, an individual can either take a regular job, enter vocational training, or continue his education in college. A resident is only permitted to do this when the leadership considers that he is ready to assume the responsibility—that he has acquired habits of punctuality, honesty, and integrity. He stays in second stage until graduation—another six months or so. After twenty months in the concept, he is closely evaluated for graduation. A graduate has the choice of living and working out as a third-stage graduate or he may live out and, if he has the proper qualifications, be eligible to join the Daytop staff. Even if he leaves, he is encouraged to stay involved with Daytop, the phrase being, "You can't keep it unless you give it away."

In conjunction with Daytop's SPAN operation, one of the most important facets of Daytop Village is the active role and support played by the Parents' Association, made up of parents and relatives of Daytop residents. It is not just a question of having parents understand what happens at Daytop. Wherever possible, the attempt is made to have parents actively confront their own emotional problems which have frequently contributed to their sons and daughters becoming prone to addiction. Encounter groups are held between families as well as between several groups of parents, and, on occasion, especially during the summer retreats to Swan Lake, parents may stay at the Fourteenth Street house in Manhattan, living as a community, themselves practicing the Daytop dynamic. Thus the parents, coming to understand and deal with their own guilt, become highly effective in working within the community, helping other parents to face the facts of addiction.

Other links between Daytop and the community include the weekly open house on Saturday nights, to which the public is invited; the speaking engagements at local churches, clinics, Rotary clubs, PTA's, and schools, and the production of the Daytop play, *The Concept,* which in addition to giving over two years of performances off-Broadway, to critical acclaim, has also played to standing ovations in cities around the country, and in Europe.

Such activities, in addition to the work performed by the lay boards of directors, trustees, and governors, headed with dedication and idealism from the start by Mngr. William B. O'Brien, contribute greatly to a public understanding of the ex-addict's problems.

It seems a long time now since that summer of 1965 when

149

my own car was rocked, stoned, and spat upon by angry demonstrators protesting the first Daytop house on Staten Island. The Daytop graduate looking for a job no longer finds himself automatically stigmatized as a dubious prospect. Word has gotten around that most graduates, with what they have learned at Daytop, and all they have at stake, make excellent workers. But, for the addicts on the street, it is still the same story. As their numbers increase, the impatience and prejudice of the public is as strong as ever. It may be that the very awareness that *some* gains have been made contributes to this hostile attitude. It is all too easy to say, "They've got therapeutic communities. They've got methadone. If they don't take advantage of such gains, they have only themselves to blame."

As this book goes to press, government aid has been cut for *all* therapeutic communities, even for methadone maintenance. In a strictly medical epidemic, no responsible government officials would conceive of stopping short at a cure rate of less than 10 percent—and it is probably closer to 5 percent—leaving the other 90 percent still infected, with the disease spreading every day. Let there be no doubt about it: psychologically, the cure for addiction is here. But, unless the public and its elected representatives have the courage and vision to go beyond half-way measures in a public health crisis so severe it defies the conventions of political and economic compromise, the epidemic can only continue to spread. Such is the broader picture in the summer of 1971, and it is, sociologically at least, far from hopeful.

DANIEL CASRIEL, M.D.

150